Lab Manual
Module B

 HOLT McDOUGAL

HOUGHTON MIFFLIN HARCOURT

Acknowledgements for Covers

Front cover: *Polar bear* (bg) ©Mark Rodger-Snelson/Alamy; *false color x-rays on hand* (l) ©Lester Lefkowitz/Getty Images; *primate* (cl) ©Bruno Morandi/The Image Bank/Getty Images; *red cells* (cr) ©Todd Davidson/Getty Images; *fossils* (r) ©Yoshihi Tanaka/amana images/Getty Images

Printed in the U.S.A.

ISBN 978-0-547-59260-2

6 7 8 9 10   2266   20 19 18 17 16
4500591409   A B C D E F G

Contents

Unit 2 Earth's Organisms

Using Your *ScienceFusion* Lab Program

Your *ScienceFusion* Lab Program is designed to include activities that address a variety of student levels, inquiry levels, time availability, and materials. In this Lab Manual, you will find that each student activity is preceded by Teacher Resources with valuable information about the activity.

Activity Type: Quick Lab

Each lesson within each unit is supported by two to three short activities called Quick Labs. Quick Labs involve simple materials and set-up. The student portion of each Quick Lab should take less than 30 minutes. Each Quick Lab includes Teacher Resources and one Student Datasheet.

Activity Types: Exploration Lab, Field Lab, and S.T.E.M. Lab

Each unit is supported by one to four additional labs that require one or more class periods to complete. Each Exploration, Field, and S.T.E.M. Lab includes Teacher Resources and two Student Datasheets. Each Student Datasheet is targeted to address different inquiry levels. Below is a description of each lab:

- **Exploration Labs** are traditional lab activities. The labs are designed to be conducted with standard laboratory equipment and materials.
- **Field Labs** are lab activities that are partially or completely performed outside the classroom or laboratory.
- **S.T.E.M. Labs** are lab activities that focus on Science, Technology, Engineering, and Math skills.

Inquiry Level

The inquiry level of each activity indicates the level at which students direct the activity. An activity that is entirely student-directed is often called Open Inquiry or Independent Inquiry. True Open or Independent Inquiry is based on a question posed by students, uses experimental processes designed by students, and requires students to find the connections between data and content. These types of activities result from student interest in the world around them. The *ScienceFusion* Lab Program provides activities that allow for a wide variety of student involvement.

- **DIRECTED Inquiry** is the least student-directed of the inquiry levels. Directed Inquiry activities provide students with an introduction to content, a procedure to follow, and direction on how to organize and analyze data.
- **GUIDED Inquiry** indicates that an activity is moderately student-directed. Guided Inquiry activities require students to select materials, procedural steps, data analysis techniques, or other aspects of the activity.
- **INDEPENDENT Inquiry** indicates that an activity is highly student-directed. Though students are provided with ideas, partial procedures, or suggestions, they are responsible for selecting many aspects of the activity.

Each Quick Lab includes one Student Datasheet that is written to support the inquiry level indicated on the Teacher Resources. Each Exploration Lab, Field Lab, and S.T.E.M. Lab includes two Student Datasheets, each written to support an inquiry level. In addition, the Teacher Resources includes one or more modification suggestions to adjust the inquiry level.

Student Level

The *ScienceFusion* Lab Program is designed to provide successful experiences for all levels of students.

- **BASIC** activities focus on introductory content and concepts taught in the lesson. These activities can be used with any level of student, including those who may have learning or language difficulties, but they may not provide a challenge for advanced students.
- **GENERAL** activities are appropriate for most students.
- **ADVANCED** activities require good understanding of the content and concepts in the lesson or ask students to manipulate content to arrive at the learning objective. Advanced activities may provide a challenge to advanced students, but they may be difficult for average or basic-level students.

Lab Ratings

Each activity is rated on three criteria to provide you with information that you may find useful when determining if an activity is appropriate for your resources.

- **Teacher Prep** rating indicates the amount of preparation you will need to provide before students can perform the activity.
- **Student Setup** rating indicates the amount of preparation students will need to perform before they begin to collect data.
- **Cleanup** rating indicates the amount of effort required to dispose of materials and disassemble the set-up of the activity.

Teacher Notes

Information and background that may be helpful to you can be found in the Teacher Notes section of the Teacher Resources. The information includes hints and a list of skills that students will practice during the activity.

Science Kit

Hands-on materials needed to complete all the labs in the Lab Manual for each module have been conveniently configured into consumable and non-consumable kits. Common materials provided by parents or your school/district are not included in the kits. Laboratory equipment commonly found in most schools has been separately packaged in a Grades 6–8 Inquiry Equipment Kit. This economical option allows schools to buy equipment only if they need it and can be shared among teachers and across grade levels. For more information on the material kits or to order, contact your local Holt McDougal sales representative or call customer service at 800-462-6595.

Online Lab Resources

The *ScienceFusion* Lab Program offers many additional resources online through our web site thinkcentral.com. These resources include:

Teacher Notes, Transparencies, and **Copymasters** are found in the Online Toolkit. Student-friendly tutorial Transparencies are available to print as transparencies or handouts. Each set of Transparencies is supported by Teacher Notes that include background information, teaching tips, and techniques. Teacher Notes, Transparencies, and Copymatsters are available to teach a broad range of skills.

- **Modeling Experimental Design** Teacher Notes and Transparencies cover Scientific Methods skills, such as Making Qualitative Observations, Developing a Hypothesis, and Making Valid Inferences.

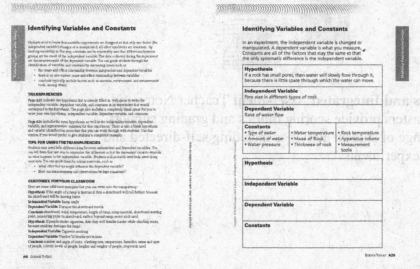

- **Writing in the Sciences** Teacher Notes and Transparencies teach written communication skills, such as Writing a Lab Report and Maintaining a Science Notebook. In addition, the Lab Report Template provides a structured format that students can use as the basis for their own lab reports.

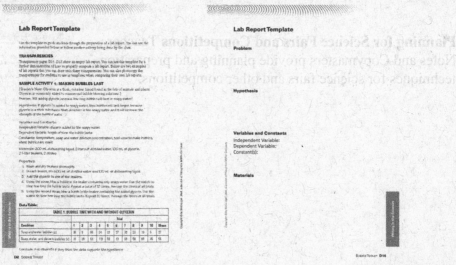

- **Math in Science Tools** Teacher Notes and Transparencies teach the math skills that are needed for data analysis in labs. These Teacher Notes and Transparencies support the S.T.E.M. concepts found throughout the *ScienceFusion* program.

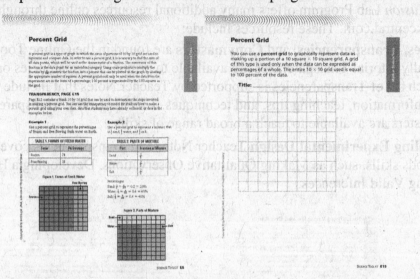

- **Rubrics and Integrated Assessment** Teacher Notes and Copymasters provide scoring rubrics and grading support for a range of student activities including self-directed and guided experiments.

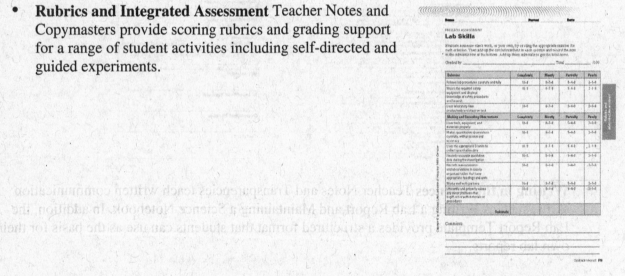

- **Planning for Science Fairs and Competitions** Teacher Notes and Copymasters provide planning and preparation techniques for science fairs and other competitions.

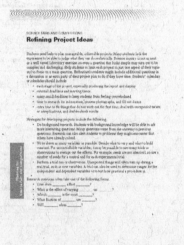

Making Your Laboratory a Safe Place

Concern for safety must begin before any activity in the classroom and before students enter the lab. A careful review of the facilities should be a basic part of preparation for each school term. You should investigate the physical environment, identify any safety risks, and inspect your work areas for compliance with safety regulations.

The review of the lab should be thorough, and all safety issues must be addressed immediately. Keep a file of your review, and add to the list each year. This will allow you to continue to raise the standard of safety in your lab and classroom.

Many classroom experiments, demonstrations, and other activities are classics that have been used for years. This familiarity may lead to a comfort that can obscure inherent safety concerns. Review all experiments, demonstrations, and activities for safety concerns before presenting them to the class. Identify and eliminate potential safety hazards.

1. **Identify the Risks** Before introducing any activity, demonstration, or experiment to the class, analyze it and consider what could possibly go wrong. Carefully review the list of materials to make sure they are safe. Inspect the equipment in your lab or classroom to make sure it is in good working order. Read the procedures to make sure they are safe. Record any hazards or concerns you identify.

2. **Evaluate the Risks** Minimize the risks you identified in the last step without sacrificing learning. Remember that no activity you perform in the lab or classroom is worth risking injury. Thus, extremely hazardous activities, or those that violate your school's policies, must be eliminated. For activities that present smaller risks, analyze each risk carefully to determine its likelihood. If the pedagogical value of the activity does not outweigh the risks, the activity must be eliminated.

3. **Select Controls to Address Risks** Even low-risk activities require controls to eliminate or minimize the risks. Make sure that in devising controls you do not substitute an equally or more hazardous alternative. Some control methods include the following:
   - Explicit verbal and written warnings may be added or posted.
   - Equipment may be rebuilt or relocated, parts may be replaced, or equipment be replaced entirely by safer alternatives.
   - Risky procedures may be eliminated.
   - Activities may be changed from student activities to teacher demonstrations.

4. **Implement and Review Selected Controls** Controls do not help if they are forgotten or not enforced. The implementation and review of controls should be as systematic and thorough as the initial analysis of safety concerns in the lab and laboratory activities.

Safety with Chemicals

Label student reagent containers with the substance's name and hazard class(es) (flammable, reactive, etc.). Dispose of hazardous waste chemicals according to federal, state, and local regulations. Refer to the MSDS for recommended disposal procedures. Remove all sources of flames, sparks, and heat from the laboratory when any flammable material is being used.

Material Safety Data Sheets

The purpose of a Material Safety Data Sheet (MSDS) is to provide readily accessible information on chemical substances commonly used in the science laboratory or in industry. The MSDS should be kept on file and referred to BEFORE handling ANY chemical. The MSDS can also be used to instruct students on chemical hazards, to evaluate spill and disposal procedures, and to warn of incompatibility with other chemicals or mixtures.

Storing Chemicals

Never store chemicals alphabetically, as this greatly increases the risk of promoting a violent reaction.

Storage Suggestions

1. Always lock the storeroom and all its cabinets when not in use.
2. Students should not be allowed in the storeroom and preparation area.
3. Avoid storing chemicals on the floor of the storeroom.
4. Do not store chemicals above eye level or on the top shelf in the storeroom.
5. Be sure shelf assemblies are firmly secured to the walls.
6. Provide anti-roll lips on all shelves.
7. Shelving should be constructed out of wood. Metal cabinets and shelves are easily corroded.
8. Avoid metal, adjustable shelf supports and clips. They can corrode, causing shelves to collapse.
9. Acids, flammables, poisons, and oxidizers should each be stored in their own locking storage cabinet.

Safety with Animals

It is recommended that teachers follow the NABT Position Statement "The Use of Animals in Biology Education" issued by the National Association of Biology Teachers (available at www.nabt.org).

Safety In Handling Preserved Materials

The following practices are recommended when handling preserved specimens:

1. NEVER dissect road-kills or nonpreserved slaughterhouse materials.
2. Wear protective gloves and splash-proof safety goggles at all times when handling preserving fluids and preserved specimens and during dissection.
3. Wear lab aprons. Use of an old shirt or smock under the lab apron is recommended.
4. Conduct dissection activities in a well-ventilated area.
5. Do not allow preservation or body-cavity fluids to contact skin. Fixatives do not distinguish between living or dead tissues. Biological supply firms may use formalin-based fixatives of varying concentrations to initially fix zoological and botanical specimens. Some provide specimens that are freezedried and rehydrated in a 10% isopropyl alcohol solution. Many suppliers provide fixed botanical materials in 50% glycerin.

Reduction Of Free Formaldehyde

Currently, federal regulations mandate a permissible exposure level of 0.75 ppm for formaldehyde. Contact your supplier for Material Data Safety Sheet (MSDS) that details the amount of formaldehyde present as well as gas-emitting characteristics for individual specimens. Prewash specimens (in a loosely covered container) in running tap water for 1–4 hours to dilute the fixative. Formaldehyde may also be chemically bound (thereby reducing danger) by immersing washed specimens in a 0.5–1.0% potassium bisulfate solution overnight or by placing them in 1% phenoxyethanol holding solutions.

Safety with Microbes

WHAT YOU CAN'T SEE CAN HURT YOU

Pathogenic (disease-causing) microorganisms are not appropriate investigation tools in the high school laboratory and should never be used.

Consult with the school nurse to screen students whose immune systems may be compromised by illness or who may be receiving immunosuppressive drug therapy. Such individuals are extraordinarily sensitive to potential infection from generally harmless microorganisms and should not participate in laboratory activities unless permitted to do so by a physician. Do not allow students who have any open cuts, abrasions, or open sores to work with microorganisms.

HOW TO USE ASEPTIC TECHNIQUE

- Demonstrate correct aseptic technique to students prior to conducting a lab activity. Never pipet liquid media by mouth. When possible, use sterile cotton applicator sticks instead of inoculating loops and Bunsen burner flames for culture inoculation. Remember to use appropriate precautions when disposing of cotton applicator sticks: they should be autoclaved or sterilized before disposal.
- Treat all microbes as pathogenic. Seal with tape all petri dishes containing bacterial cultures. Do not use blood agar plates, and never attempt to cultivate microbes from a human or animal source.
- Never dispose of microbe cultures without sterilizing them first. Autoclave or steam-sterilize at 120°C and 15 psi for 15 to 20 minutes all used cultures and any materials that have come in contact with them. If these devices are not available, flood or immerse these articles in full-strength household bleach for 30 minutes, and then discard. Use the autoclave or steam sterilizer yourself; do not allow students to use these devices.
- Wash all lab surfaces with a disinfectant solution before and after handling bacterial cultures.

HOW TO HANDLE BACTERIOLOGICAL SPILLS

- Never allow students to clean up bacteriological spills. Keep on hand a spill kit containing 500 mL of full-strength household bleach, biohazard bags (autoclavable), forceps, and paper towels.
- In the event of a bacterial spill, cover the area with a layer of paper towels. Wet the paper towels with bleach, and allow them to stand for 15 to 20 minutes. Wearing gloves and using forceps, place the residue in the biohazard bag. If broken glass is present, use a brush and dustpan to collect material, and place it in a suitably marked puncture-resistant container for disposal.

Personal Protective Equipment

Chemical goggles (Meeting ANSI Standard Z87.1) These should be worn with any chemical or chemical solution other than water, when heating substances, using any mechanical device, or observing physical processes that could eject an object.

Face shield (Meeting ANSI Standard Z87.1) Use in combination with eye goggles when working with corrosives.

Contact lenses The wearing of contact lenses for cosmetic reasons should be prohibited in the laboratory. If a student must wear contact lenses prescribed by a physician, that student should be instructed to wear eye-cup safety goggles, similar to swimmer's cup goggles, meeting ANSI Standard Z87.1.

Eye-wash station The device must be capable of delivering a copious, gentle flow of water to both eyes for at least 15 minutes. Portable liquid supply devices are not satisfactory and should not be used. A plumbed-in fixture or a perforated spray head on the end of a hose attached to a plumbed-in outlet is suitable if it is designed for use as an eye-wash fountain and meets ANSI Standard Z358.1. It must be within a 30-second walking distance from any spot in the room.

Safety shower (Meeting ANSI Standard Z358.1) Location should be within a 30-second walking distance from any spot in the room. Students should be instructed in the use of the safety shower in the event of a fire or chemical splash on their body that cannot simply be washed off.

Gloves Polyethylene, neoprene rubber, or disposable plastic may be used. Nitrile or butyl rubber gloves are recommended when handling corrosives.

Apron Rubber-coated cloth or vinyl (nylon-coated) halter is recommended.

Student Safety in the Laboratory

Systematic, careful lab work is an essential part of any science program. The equipment and apparatus students will use present various safety hazards. You must be aware of these hazards before students engage in any lab activity. The Teacher Resource Pages at the beginning of each lab in this Lab Manual will guide you in properly directing the equipment use during the experiments. Photocopy the information on the following pages for students. These safety rules always apply in the lab and in the field.

Safety Symbols

The following safety symbols will appear in the instructions for labs and activities to emphasize important notes of caution. Learn what they represent so that you can take the appropriate precautions.

	Eye Protection • Wear approved safety goggles at all times in the lab as directed. • If chemicals get into your eyes, flush your eyes immediately. • Do not wear contact lenses in the lab. • Do not look directly at the sun or any intense light source or laser.
	Hand Safety • Do not cut an object while holding the object in your hand. • Wear appropriate protective gloves when working with an open flame, chemicals, solutions, or wild or unknown plants. • Use a heat-resistant mitt to handle equipment that may be hot.
	Clothing Protection • Wear an apron or lab coat at all times in the lab. • Tie back long hair, secure loose clothing, and remove loose jewelry so that they do not knock over equipment, get caught in moving parts, or come into contact with hazardous materials or electrical connections. • Do not wear open-toed shoes, sandals, or canvas shoes in the lab. • When outside for lab, wear long sleeves, long pants, socks, and closed shoes.
	Glassware Safety • Inspect glassware before use; do not use chipped or cracked glassware. • Use heat-resistant glassware for heating materials or storing hot liquids. • Notify your teacher immediately if a piece of glassware or a light bulb breaks.
	Sharp-Object Safety • Use extreme care when handling all sharp and pointed instruments. • Cut objects on a suitable surface, always in a direction away from your body. • Be aware of sharp objects or edges on equipment or apparatus.
	Chemical Safety • If a chemical gets on your skin, on your clothing, or in your eyes, rinse it immediately (shower, faucet or eyewash fountain) and alert your teacher. • Do not clean up spilled chemicals yourself unless your teacher directs you to do so. • Do not inhale any gas or vapor unless your teacher directs you to do so. • Handle materials that emit vapors or gases in a well-ventilated area.

Name _____ Class _____ Date _____

Electrical Safety
- Do not use equipment with frayed electrical cords or loose plugs.
- Fasten electrical cords to work surfaces by using tape.
- Do not use electrical equipment near water or when clothing or hands are wet.
- Hold the plug housing when you plug in or unplug equipment.
- Be aware that wire coils in electrical circuits may heat up rapidly.

Heating Safety
- Be aware of any source of flames, sparks, or heat (such as open flames, heating coils, or hot plates) before working with any flammable substances.
- Avoid using open flames.
- Know the location of lab fire extinguishers and fire-safety blankets.
- Know your school's fire-evacuation routes.
- If your clothing catches on fire, walk to the lab shower to put out the fire.
- Never leave a hot plate unattended while it is turned on or while it is cooling.
- Use tongs or appropriate insulated holders when handling heated objects.
- Allow all equipment to cool before storing it.

Plant Safety
- Do not eat any part of a plant or plant seed.
- When outside, do not pick any wild plants unless your teacher instructs you to do so.
- Wash your hands thoroughly after handling any part of a plant.

Animal Safety
- Handle animals only as your teacher directs.
- Treat animals carefully and respectfully.
- Wash your hands thoroughly after handling any animal.

Proper Waste Disposal
- Clean and sanitize all work surfaces and personal protective equipment after each lab period as directed by your teacher.
- Dispose of hazardous materials only as directed by your teacher.
- Dispose of sharp objects (such as broken glass) in the appropriate sharps or broken glass container as directed by your teacher.

Hygienic Care
- Keep your hands away from your face while you are working on any activity.
- Wash your hands thoroughly before you leave the lab or after any activity.
- Remove contaminated clothing immediately.

Safety in the Laboratory

1. **Always wear a lab apron and safety goggles.** Wear these safety devices whenever you are in the lab, not just when you are working on an experiment.

2. **No contact lenses in the lab.** Contact lenses should not be worn during any investigations in which you are using chemicals (even if you are wearing goggles). In the event of an accident, chemicals can get behind contact lenses and cause serious damage before the lenses can be removed. If your doctor requires that you wear contact lenses instead of glasses, you should wear eye-cup safety goggles in the lab. Ask your doctor or your teacher how to use this very important and special eye protection.

3. **Personal apparel should be appropriate for laboratory work.** On lab days, avoid wearing long necklaces, dangling bracelets, bulky jewelry, and bulky or loose-fitting clothing. Long hair should be tied back. Loose, flopping, or dangling items may get caught in moving parts, accidentally contact electrical connections, or interfere with the investigation in some potentially hazardous manner. In addition, chemical fumes may react with some jewelry, such as pearls, and ruin them. Cotton clothing is preferable to wool, nylon, or polyesters. Wear shoes that will protect your feet from chemical spills and falling objects— no open-toed shoes or sandals and no shoes with woven leather straps.

4. **NEVER work alone in the laboratory.** Work in the lab only while supervised by your teacher. Do not leave equipment unattended while it is in operation.

5. **Only books and notebooks needed for the activity should be in the lab.** Only the lab notebook and perhaps the textbook should be used. Keep other books, backpacks, purses, and similar items in your desk, locker, or designated storage area.

6. **Read the entire activity before entering the lab.** Your teacher will review any applicable safety precautions before you begin the lab activity. If you are not sure of something, ask your teacher about it.

7. Always heed safety symbols and cautions in the instructions for the experiments, in handouts, and on posters in the room, and always heed cautions given verbally by your teacher. They are provided for your safety.

8. Know the proper fire drill procedures and the locations of fire exits and emergency equipment. Make sure you know the procedures to follow in case of a fire or other emergency.

9. **If your clothing catches on fire, do not run;** WALK to the safety shower, stand under the showerhead, and turn the water on. Call to your teacher while you do this.

10. **Report all accidents to the teacher** IMMEDIATELY, no matter how minor. In addition, if you get a headache or feel ill or dizzy, tell your teacher immediately.

Safety in the Laboratory continued

11. **Report all spills to your teacher immediately.** Call your teacher, rather than cleaning a spill yourself. Your teacher will tell you if it is safe for you to clean up the spill. If it is not safe for you to clean up the spill, your teacher will know how the spill should be cleaned up safely.

12. If a lab directs you to design your own experiments, procedures must be approved by your teacher BEFORE you begin work.

13. DO NOT perform unauthorized experiments or use equipment or apparatus in a manner for which they were not intended. Use only materials and equipment listed in the activity equipment list or authorized by your teacher. Steps in a procedure should only be performed as described in the lab manual or as approved by your teacher.

14. **Stay alert while in the lab, and proceed with caution.** Be aware of others near you or your equipment when you are proceeding with the experiment. If you are not sure of how to proceed, ask your teacher for help.

15. **Horseplay in the lab is very dangerous.** Laboratory equipment and apparatus are not toys; never play in the lab or use lab time or equipment for anything other than their intended purpose.

16. Food, beverages, and chewing gum are NEVER permitted in the laboratory.

17. **NEVER taste chemicals.** Do not touch chemicals or allow them to contact areas of bare skin.

18. **Use extreme CAUTION when working with hot plates or other heating devices.** Keep your head, hands, hair, and clothing away from the flame or heating area, and turn the devices off when they are not in use. Remember that metal surfaces connected to the heated area will become hot by conduction. Gas burners should be lit only with a spark lighter. Make sure all heating devices and gas valves are turned off before leaving the laboratory. Never leave a hot plate or other heating device unattended when it is in use. Remember that many metal, ceramic, and glass items do not always look hot when they are heated. Allow all items to cool before storing them.

19. **Exercise caution when working with electrical equipment.** Do not use electrical equipment that has frayed or twisted wires. Be sure your hands are dry before you use electrical equipment. Do not let electrical cords dangle from work stations; dangling cords can cause tripping or electrical shocks.

20. **Keep work areas and apparatus clean and neat.** Always clean up any clutter made during the course of lab work, rearrange apparatus in an orderly manner, and report any damaged or missing items.

21. Always thoroughly wash your hands with soap and water at the conclusion of each investigation.

Safety in the Field

Activities conducted outdoors require some advance planning to ensure a safe environment. The following general guidelines should be followed for fieldwork.

1. **Know your mission.** Your teacher will tell you the goal of the field trip in advance. Be sure to have your permission slip approved before the trip, and check to be sure that you have all necessary supplies for the day's activity.

2. **Find out about on-site hazards before setting out.** Determine whether poisonous plants or dangerous animals are likely to be present where you are going. Know how to identify these hazards. Find out about other hazards, such as steep or slippery terrain.

3. **Wear protective clothing.** Dress in a manner that will keep you warm, comfortable, and dry. Decide in advance whether you will need sunglasses, a hat, gloves, boots, or rain gear to suit the terrain and local weather conditions.

4. **Do not approach or touch wild animals.** If you see a threatening animal, call your teacher immediately. Avoid any living thing that may sting, bite, scratch, or otherwise cause injury.

5. **Do not touch wild plants or pick wildflowers unless specifically instructed to do so** by your teacher. Many wild plants can be irritating or toxic. Never taste any wild plant.

6. **Do not wander away from others.** Travel with a partner at all times. Stay within an area where you can be seen or heard in case you run into trouble.

7. **Report all hazards or accidents to your teacher immediately.** Even if the incident seems unimportant, let your teacher know what happened.

8. **Maintain the safety of the environment.** Do not remove anything from the field site without your teacher's permission. Stay on trails, when possible, to avoid trampling delicate vegetation. Never leave garbage behind at a field site. Leave natural areas as you found them.

Laboratory Techniques

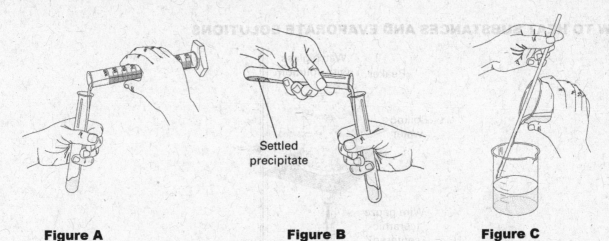

Settled
precipitate

Figure A   **Figure B**   **Figure C**

HOW TO DECANT AND TRANSFER LIQUIDS

1. The safest way to transfer a liquid from a graduated cylinder to a test tube is shown in **Figure A**. The liquid is transferred at arm's length, with the elbows slightly bent. This position enables you to see what you are doing while maintaining steady control of the equipment.

2. Sometimes, liquids contain particles of insoluble solids that sink to the bottom of a test tube or beaker. Use one of the methods shown above to separate a supernatant (the clear fluid) from insoluble solids.

   a. **Figure B** shows the proper method of decanting a supernatant liquid from a test tube.

   b. **Figure C** shows the proper method of decanting a supernatant liquid from a beaker by using a stirring rod. The rod should touch the wall of the receiving container. Hold the stirring rod against the lip of the beaker containing the supernatant. As you pour, the liquid will run down the rod and fall into the beaker resting below. When you use this method, the liquid will not run down the side of the beaker from which you are pouring.

Laboratory Techniques continued

HOW TO HEAT SUBSTANCES AND EVAPORATE SOLUTIONS

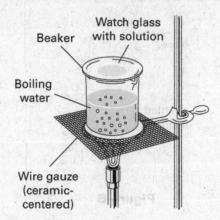

FIGURE D

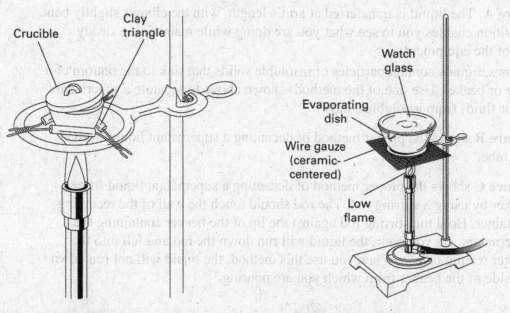

FIGURE E   **FIGURE F**

1. Use care in selecting glassware for high-temperature heating. The glassware should be heat resistant.

2. When heating glassware by using a gas flame, use a ceramic-centered wire gauze to protect glassware from direct contact with the flame. Wire gauzes can withstand extremely high temperatures and will help prevent glassware from breaking. **Figure D** shows the proper setup for evaporating a solution over a water bath.

3. In some experiments, you are required to heat a substance to high temperatures in a porcelain crucible. Figure E shows the proper apparatus setup used to accomplish this task.

4. **Figure F** shows the proper setup for evaporating a solution in a porcelain evaporating dish with a watch glass cover that prevents spattering.

Laboratory Techniques continued

5. Glassware, porcelain, and iron rings that have been heated may look cool after they are removed from a heat source, but these items can still burn your skin even after several minutes of cooling. Use tongs, test-tube holders, or heat-resistant mitts and pads whenever you handle these pieces of apparatus.

6. You can test the temperature of beakers, ring stands, wire gauzes, or other pieces of apparatus that have been heated by holding the back of your hand close to their surfaces before grasping them. You will be able to feel any energy as heat generated from the hot surfaces. DO NOT TOUCH THE APPARATUS. Allow plenty of time for the apparatus to cool before handling.

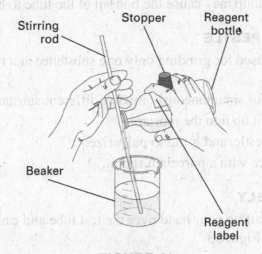

FIGURE G

HOW TO POUR LIQUID FROM A REAGENT BOTTLE

1. Read the label at least three times before using the contents of a reagent bottle.

2. Never lay the stopper of a reagent bottle on the lab table.

3. When pouring a caustic or corrosive liquid into a beaker, use a stirring rod to avoid drips and spills. Hold the stirring rod against the lip of the reagent bottle. Estimate the amount of liquid you need, and pour this amount along the rod, into the beaker. See **Figure G**.

4. Extra precaution should be taken when handling a bottle of acid. Remember the following important rules: Never add water to any concentrated acid, particularly sulfuric acid, because the mixture can splash and will generate a lot of energy as heat. To dilute any acid, add the acid to water in small quantities while stirring slowly. Remember the "triple A's"—*Always Add Acid* to water.

5. Examine the outside of the reagent bottle for any liquid that has dripped down the bottle or spilled on the counter top. Your teacher will show you the proper procedures for cleaning up a chemical spill.

6. Never pour reagents back into stock bottles. At the end of the experiment, your teacher will tell you how to dispose of any excess chemicals.

Laboratory Techniques continued

HOW TO HEAT MATERIAL IN A TEST TUBE

1. Check to see that the test tube is heat resistant.
2. Always use a test tube holder or clamp when heating a test tube.
3. Never point a heated test tube at anyone, because the liquid may splash out of the test tube.
4. Never look down into the test tube while heating it.
5. Heat the test tube from the upper portions of the tube downward, and continuously move the test tube, as shown in **Figure H**. Do not heat any one spot on the test tube. Otherwise, a pressure buildup may cause the bottom of the tube to blow out.

HOW TO USE A MORTAR AND PESTLE

1. A mortar and pestle should be used for grinding only one substance at a time. See **Figure I**.
2. Never use a mortar and pestle for simultaneously mixing different substances.
3. Place the substance to be broken up into the mortar.
4. Pound the substance with the pestle, and grind to pulverize.
5. Remove the powdered substance with a porcelain spoon.

HOW TO DETECT ODORS SAFELY

1. Test for the odor of gases by wafting your hand over the test tube and cautiously sniffing the fumes as shown in **Figure J**.
2. Do not inhale any fumes directly.
3. Use a fume hood whenever poisonous or irritating fumes are present. DO NOT waft and sniff poisonous or irritating fumes.

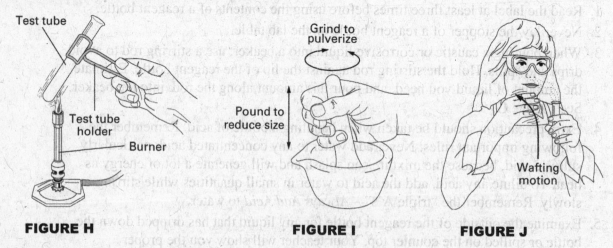

FIGURE H

FIGURE I

FIGURE J

Original content Copyright © by Holt McDougal. Alterations to the original content are the responsibility of the instructor.

Student Safety Quiz

Circle the letter of the BEST answer.

1. Before starting an investigation or lab procedure, you should

    a. try an experiment of your own

    b. open all containers and packages

    c. read all directions and make sure you understand them

    d. handle all the equipment to become familiar with it

2. When pouring chemicals between containers, you should hold the containers over

    a. the floor or a waste basket

    b. a fire blanket or an oven mitt

    c. an eyewash station or a water fountain

    d. a sink or your work area

3. If you get hurt or injured in any way, you should

    a. tell your teacher immediately

    b. find bandages or a first aid kit

    c. go to the principal's office

    d. get help after you finish the lab

4. If your glassware is chipped or broken, you should

    a. use it only for solid materials

    b. give it to your teacher

    c. put it back into the storage cabinet

    d. increase the damage so that it is obvious

5. If you have unused chemicals after finishing a procedure, you should

    a. pour them down a sink or drain

    b. mix them all together in a bucket

    c. put them back into their original containers

    d. throw them away where your teacher tells you to

Name _____ Class _____ Date _____

6. If electrical equipment has a frayed cord, you should

   a. unplug the equipment by pulling on the cord

   b. let the cord hang over the side of a counter or table

   c. tell your teacher about the problem immediately

   d. wrap tape around the cord to repair it

7. If you need to determine the odor of a chemical or a solution, you should

   a. use your hand to bring fumes from the container to your nose

   b. bring the container under your nose and inhale deeply

   c. tell your teacher immediately

   d. use odor-sensing equipment

8. When working with materials that might fly into the air and hurt someone's eye, you should wear

   a. goggles

   b. an apron

   c. gloves

   d. a hat

9. Before doing experiments involving a heat source, you should know the location of the

   a. door

   b. windows

   c. fire extinguisher

   d. overhead lights

10. If you get a chemical in your eye, you should

   a. wash your hands immediately

   b. put the lid back on the chemical container

   c. wait to see if your eye becomes irritated

   d. use the eyewash right away

11. When working with a flame or heat source, you should

    a. tie back long hair or hair that hangs in front of your eyes

    b. heat substances or objects inside a closed container

    c. touch an object with your bare hand to see how hot it is

    d. throw hot objects into the trash when you are done with them

12. As you cut with a knife or other sharp instrument, you should move the instrument

    a. toward you

    b. away from you

    c. vertically

    d. horizontally

LAB SAFETY QUIZ
Answer Key

1. C	5. D	9. C
2. D	6. C	10. D
3. A	7. A	11. A
4. B	8. A	12. B

Student Safety Contract

Read carefully the Student Safety Contract below. Then, fill in your name in the first blank, date the contract, and sign it.

Student Safety Contract

I will
- read the lab investigation before coming to class
- wear personal protective equipment as directed to protect my eyes, face, hands, and body while conducting class activities
- follow all instructions given by the teacher
- conduct myself in a responsible manner at all times in a laboratory situation

I, _____, have read and agree to abide by the safety regulations as set forth above and any additional printed instructions provided by my teacher or the school district.

I agree to follow all other written and oral instructions given in class.

Signature: _____

Date: _____

QUICK LAB GUIDED Inquiry

Is a Clock Alive? BASIC

👥 Small groups

🕐 15 minutes

LAB RATINGS

Teacher Prep —

Student Setup —

Cleanup —

LESS ←——————→ MORE

MATERIALS

For each group
• analog clock
• paper, plain
  (8 1/2" × 11"
  or larger)

SAFETY INFORMATION

Remind students to review all safety cautions and icons before beginning this lab.

My Notes
_____
_____
_____
_____
_____

TEACHER NOTES

In this activity, students will investigate living and nonliving things. They will observe a clock and use a graphic organizer to assist in comparing the characteristics of the clock with the characteristics of an animal.

Tip This activity will help students understand the differences and similarities between living and nonliving things.

Student Tip Think about what it means to be alive, and what conditions something has to meet to be considered alive.

Skills Focus Making Comparisons, Drawing Conclusions, Making a Graphic Organizer

MODIFICATION FOR INDEPENDENT Inquiry

Challenge the students to determine what characteristics something must exhibit to be considered a living thing. Have students select two objects for comparison (such as clock, ball, cat, dog, lamp, computer, or horse). Using a graphic organizer of their choice and an oral presentation, students demonstrate the characteristics they selected, and explain whether or not their two objects are living or nonliving.

Answer Key for GUIDED Inquiry

1. Accept all reasonable answers, but look for students to recognize the following basic characteristics: takes energy from another source, grows, reproduces, capable of movement, responds to stimuli, composed of cells, produces wastes.

Quick Lab continued

2. Accept all reasonable answers. Sample answer: The clock can move, but it can not move by itself and it moves in a limited and defined range. It uses energy from the environment, but it can not get that energy by itself. It does not reproduce or respond to stimuli in the environment. It does not grow, either.

Teacher Prompt How does the clock move? How does it get energy? Can it reproduce on its own? Will it get bigger as it gets older?

3. Sample answer:

Clock	Characteristic	Animals
Yes, but it is limited in range and only the hands can move	Moves	Yes, they can fly, swim, run, climb and do these things without help
No	Eats and drinks	Yes
No	Sleeps	Yes
Yes, they use batteries or electric power	Uses energy	Yes, they use food and drink
No	Reproduces	Yes
No	Responds to outside stimuli	Yes
No	Made of cells	Yes

4. Sample answer: According to the characteristics our group described for living things, a clock is clearly not a living thing. Although it moves, it doesn't decide where it's going to move, or for what purpose. Clocks do not use food or drink for energy like animals. Animals can have offspring, but only clockmakers can make more clocks. Also, an animal will respond to stimuli, like a loud clap, or the smell of food, and a clock will not. Clearly, clocks are not animals.

Teacher Prompt Is a clock a living thing? What must all living things do or have? Do clocks do or have those things?

QUICK LAB GUIDED (Inquiry)

QUICK LAB GUIDED (Inquiry)

Is a Clock Alive?

In this lab, you will compare the characteristics of a clock with the characteristics of an animal and create a graphic organizer to compare and contrast these characteristics.

OBJECTIVES

- Observe the characteristics of a clock.
- Compare the characteristics of a clock to those of an animal.

MATERIALS

For each group
- analog clock
- paper, plain (8 1/2" × 11" or larger)

PROCEDURE

❶ In your group, discuss the characteristics that distinguish living things from nonliving things. Write a list below that includes all of the characteristics your group decided on.

_____

_____

_____

_____

❷ Take a few minutes to observe the clock. How many of the characteristics that you listed in the first step apply to the clock? Explain each one below.

_____

_____

_____

_____

❸ Choose a type of graphic organizer that can compare and contrast the characteristics of the clock with the characteristics of an animal. Use the white paper to create your graphic organizer.

❹ In a paragraph on the back of your graphic organizer, explain why a clock is or is not a living thing based on evidence from your observations during this investigation.

QUICK LAB GUIDED *Inquiry*

The Needs of Producers, Consumers, and Decomposers GENERAL

MATERIALS
For each group
• paper
• scissors
• string
• tape

🐾 Small groups
🕐 15 minutes

LAB RATINGS

LESS ← → MORE

Teacher Prep —

Student Setup —

Cleanup —

My Notes

_____

_____

_____

_____

_____

SAFETY INFORMATION

Remind students to review all safety cautions and icons before beginning this lab.

TEACHER NOTES

In this activity, students will identify the needs of living things and describe specific examples of the needs of producers, consumers, and decomposers.

Tip This activity will help students understand that living things have specific needs for water, food, energy, and habitat in order to survive.

Student Tip Think about the things your body needs to survive. What types of survival needs are shared by most organisms?

Skills Focus Drawing Conclusions, Creating a Graphic Organizer, Making Comparisons

MODIFICATION FOR INDEPENDENT *Inquiry*

Challenge students to create a presentation on producers, consumers, and decomposers. Students in small groups may use classroom resources to develop a definition and examples for each category, and to determine what needs are common and unique among them. They should present their findings in an oral presentation accompanied by a graphic organizer of their choice. Provide them the same materials listed above.

Answer Key

1. You may wish to provide students with a list of organisms from each of the three groups from which to select to ensure they make a correct selection. Alternatively, you may have other group members check each student's selection, or require students to get your approval on the organism they selected before they begin Step 2.

2. Sample answer: a student assigned "producer" selects a "rose," and the needs include: sunlight, water, soil, and warm climate.

4. Sample answer:

Cow	Category	Sunflower
Corn, grass	Energy	Sunlight and nutrients in soil.
Can move to water source	Water	Can not move to water source
Farms, pastures	Habitat	Sunny, open places; rooted to ground

Name _____ Class _____ Date _____

The Needs of Producers, Consumers, and Decomposers

In this lab, you will create a web that shows the needs of living things and gives specific examples of the needs of producers, consumers, and decomposers.

PROCEDURE

1 Your teacher will assign your group to study a producer, consumer, or decomposer. Each student will choose a particular organism from your assigned category and write it on a slip of paper.

2 Next, each student in your group will identify four specific needs that the organism depends on for survival. Consider categories of needs such as

- water
- food
- energy
- habitat

Write each of the four needs on individual slips of paper.

3 Use the slips, scissors, string, and tape to create a "web" that illustrates the relationship between the organism and its needs.

4 Then, students take turns explaining their web to other group members. After each student has presented their web, the small group will select two or more organisms and create a graphic organizer that shows similarities and differences in their needs.

OBJECTIVES

- Identify the needs of living things.
- Describe specific examples of the needs of producers, consumers, and decomposers.

MATERIALS

For each group
- paper
- scissors
- string
- tape

Poster
group of
4

Lighthouse Youth Center
245 Commerce Street • P.O. Box 38
Oxford, PA 19363
610-467-6000

QUICK LAB DIRECTED Inquiry

Model Natural Selection GENERAL

👥 Student pairs
🕐 15 minutes

LAB RATINGS

LESS ◄─────────► MORE

Teacher Prep —

Student Setup —

Cleanup —

MATERIALS

For each student pair
- cloth, white, approximately 20 cm × 20 cm
- marshmallows, colored (all same color), miniature (25)
- marshmallows, white, miniature (25)

SAFETY INFORMATION

Remind students that they should never ingest any lab materials.

My Notes

_____

_____

_____

_____

_____

TEACHER NOTES

In this activity, students will use a white cloth and either white or colored marshmallows to create a simple model of natural selection. Newspaper can be used as an alternative to marshmallows in this activity. Instead of using marshmallows, use a hole punch to punch 25 holes from the classified section of a newspaper and 25 holes from newsprint in multiple colors, such as the Sunday comics. Instead of using cloth, use the newspaper for the background. Spread the holes on the paper, and have the "hunter" pick up as many as he or she can in 15 seconds. Tally the results.

Skills Focus Interpreting Results, Applying Concepts

MODIFICATION FOR INDEPENDENT Inquiry

Have students investigate natural selection. Students should formulate a testable question or explanation based on their research. Students should conduct a fair and unbiased test of their question or explanation. Finally, students should communicate the procedures and results of their investigations and explanations to the class.

Answer Key

4. Answers will vary, but students are likely to pick up more colored marshmallows than white ones.

5. Sample answer: The marshmallows represent organisms that could be eaten; the cloth represents the area where they live.

6. Sample answer: Many organisms in the wild blend into their surroundings by having colors or patterns that make them hard to see. This might help them hide from things trying to eat them. A weakness of this model is that it's very simple—a real "wild" environment would be more than two colors and would contain a variety of organisms.

QUICK LAB DIRECTED *Inquiry*

Model Natural Selection

In this activity, you will see how traits can affect the success of an organism in a particular environment.

PROCEDURE

❶ Count out **25 colored marshmallows** and **25 white marshmallows.**

❷ Ask your partner to look away while you spread the marshmallows out on a **white cloth.** Do not make a pattern with the marshmallows. Now, ask your partner to turn around and pick the first marshmallow that he or she sees. Record your result in the table below.

❸ Repeat Step 2 ten times. Record your results in the table below.

MARSHMALLOW HUNT RESULTS

Attempt	1	2	3	4	5
Color of marshmallow					
Attempt	6	7	8	9	10
Color of marshmallow					

❹ How many white marshmallows did your partner pick? How many colored marshmallows did he or she pick?

Total of white marshmallows: _____

Total of colored marshmallows: _____

❺ What did the marshmallows and the cloth represent in your investigation? What effect did the color of the cloth have?

_____

_____

_____

_____

_____

_____

OBJECTIVES

- Make a simple model of camouflage.
- Describe how coloration can affect the survival of an organism.

MATERIALS

For each student pair
- cloth, white, approximately 20 cm × 20 cm
- marshmallows, colored (all same color), miniature (25)
- marshmallows, white, miniature (25)

Quick Lab continued

6 When an organism blends into its environment, the organism is *camouflaged*. How does this activity model camouflaged organisms in the wild? What are some weaknesses of this model?

_____

_____

_____

_____

_____

_____

QUICK LAB GUIDED Inquiry

Analyzing Survival Adaptations ADVANCED

🐾 Individual student

🕐 20 minutes

LAB RATINGS

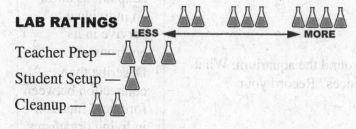

LESS ←——————→ MORE

Teacher Prep —

Student Setup —

Cleanup —

MATERIALS

For each student

- aquarium containing live fish
- colored pencils or markers
- habitat information of aquarium fish
- paper, blank

SAFETY INFORMATION

Remind students to review all safety cautions and icons before beginning this lab.

TEACHER NOTES

In this activity, students will compare and contrast two species of fish by assessing the survival advantages offered by various adaptations. Students will then determine adaptations that would help a fish survive in given habitat.

Provide the students with an information sheet about each species of fish in the aquarium. Include specific information on the native habitat of each species. If fish specimens are not available, pictures of fish obtained from magazines or the Internet can also be used.

Skills Focus Making Observations, Applying Concepts, Making Predictions

My Notes

_____

_____

_____

_____

_____

MODIFICATION FOR INDEPENDENT Inquiry

Have students learn about the kinds of adaptations that fish have. They should consider the features of a fish's environment that might cause adaptations in a species. Students should summarize their findings and present them to the class.

Answer Key

1. Sample answer: Both have fins and gills. Fish 1 is brown and has a long, slender body and side fins. Fish 2 has bright colors, fins against its body, and is thin.

2. Sample answer: Both native habitats have water. Fish 1 lives in flowing waters. Fish 2 lives near a reef.

3. Sample answer: Fish 1 blends into its habitat using its color and flat shape. It uses its side fins to help move through mud. These would camouflage it to avoid predators.

4. Sample answer: Fish 2 uses its color to blend into the reef, and its thin shape and fins against its sides allow it to fit into small spaces. This would let it hide from predators.

5. Answers will vary.

QUICK LAB GUIDED Inquiry

Analyzing Survival Adaptations

In this lab, you will learn about adaptations that help fish survive in different habitats.

PROCEDURE

1 Observe the two fish as they move around the aquarium. What similarities do you see? What differences? Record your observations.

_____

_____

_____

_____

_____

_____

_____

2 Study the information on the native habitat of the first fish. How is it similar to the habitat of the second fish? How is it different? Record your observations.

_____

_____

_____

_____

_____

_____

_____

_____

OBJECTIVES

- Describe how adaptations allow an individual to survive in its environment.
- Describe the connection between form and function in living organisms.

MATERIALS

For each student
- aquarium containing live fish
- colored pencils or markers
- habitat information of aquarium fish
- paper, blank

Quick Lab continued

❸ Describe how you think the first fish uses its fins, color, and shape to
survive in its habitat. What are the advantages of these adaptations?

_____

_____

_____

_____

_____

_____

❹ Describe how you think the second fish uses its fins, color, and shape to
survive in its habitat. What are the advantages of these adaptations?

_____

_____

_____

_____

_____

_____

❺ List 3 adaptations a fish might have if it lived in a mangrove forest. On a
separate piece of paper, use **colored pencils or markers** to draw a picture
of a fish with those adaptations. Describe how each adaptation would be an
advantage in this new habitat.

_____

_____

_____

_____

_____

_____

_____

QUICK LAB GUIDED Inquiry

The Opposable Thumb GENERAL

👥 Small groups
🕐 20 minutes

LAB RATINGS

LESS ⟵——————⟶ MORE

Teacher Prep —

Student Setup —

Cleanup —

MATERIALS

For each group
- bag, zip-top
- book
- clay
- fork, plastic
- knife, plastic
- paper
- pencil
- plate, paper
- scissors
- stopwatch
- tape

For each student
- safety goggles

SAFETY INFORMATION

Remind students to review all safety cautions and icons before beginning this lab.

TEACHER NOTES

In this lab, students learn about the importance of the opposable thumb to primates. Activities such as buttoning a shirt and eating dinner demonstrate that the simplest of daily activities are possible only because of opposable thumbs.

Skills Focus Making Observations, Evaluating Results, Drawing Conclusions

My Notes

_____

_____

_____

_____

_____

MODIFICATION FOR DIRECTED Inquiry

At Step 3, provide a process for the group that identifies each individual's role and defines how the time to accomplish a task will be measured and recorded.

MODIFICATION FOR INDEPENDENT Inquiry

Have students use the Internet to learn about robotic appendages used to replace lost limbs. Students should specifically identify the benefits and drawbacks of robotic appendages.

Answer Key

3. Answers may vary.

4. Answers may vary. Students should recognize that the testers themselves are variables because different students may perform each task at a different rate.

5. Answers may vary.

6. Answers may vary.

7. Answers may vary.

Quick Lab continued

8. Accept all reasonable answers. In general, tasks should be harder to do without the use of thumbs. However, certain tasks may be easier than others.
Teacher Prompt Encourage students to identify factors other than speed that might indicate how easy a task was.

9. Answers may vary.

10. Sample answer: The simplest of human daily activities are possible only because of our opposable thumbs. Grasping hands allow humans to manipulate tools and our environment with ease.

QUICK LAB GUIDED *Inquiry*

The Opposable Thumb

In this activity, you will learn how an opposable thumb helps you perform everyday tasks.

PROCEDURE

❶ Work in groups of three students.

❷ For each task below, one student will be the timekeeper, one student will be a tester using thumbs, and one student will be a tester without using thumbs. The tester without using thumbs will need to use **tape** to connect his or her thumb to the second finger of each hand.

❸ Within your group, decide how you will split up roles and tasks. Your plan must include recording the time it takes to accomplish each task using thumbs and without using thumbs. Record your plan.

_____

_____

_____

_____

❹ Is your plan a controlled experiment? Why or why not?

_____

_____

_____

❺ Perform the following tasks and record the time:

Open and close a **zip-top bag.**

_____

Open a **book** and turn to page 52.

_____

Use a **pencil** to write *thumb*.

_____

Tear off a small piece of tape.

_____

OBJECTIVES

- Describe the role of the opposable thumb in performing everyday tasks.
- Describe the importance of the opposable thumb as a physical characteristic.

MATERIALS

For each group
- bag, zip-top
- book
- clay
- fork, plastic
- knife, plastic
- paper
- pencil
- plate, paper
- scissors
- stopwatch
- tape

For each student
- safety goggles

Quick Lab continued

Use **scissors** to cut a circle from a **sheet of paper.**

_____

Put the **clay** on a **plate.** Use a **fork** and **knife** to cut the clay into 10 small pieces.

_____

6 Calculate the total amount of time it took to complete the tasks with and without using thumbs.

_____

7 Did the testers without opposable thumbs have to do tasks differently from testers who used their thumbs? Explain.

_____

_____

_____

8 Were all of the tasks equally difficult without an opposable thumb? Why might some tasks be more difficult than others?

_____

_____

_____

9 Other than the tasks in this activity, what are some actions that would be difficult or impossible without opposable thumbs?

_____

_____

_____

10 How do opposable thumbs give primates an advantage over animals without opposable thumbs?

_____

_____

_____

EXPLORATION LAB DIRECTED *Inquiry* **OR** GUIDED *Inquiry*

Environmental Change and Evolution ADVANCED

👥 Small groups
🕐 45 minutes

LAB RATINGS

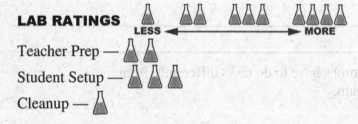

LESS ◄──────────► MORE

Teacher Prep —

Student Setup —

Cleanup —

MATERIALS

For each group
- aluminum foil
- cotton balls or batting
- feathers, different sizes
- felt or cloth
- glue
- marker, permanent
- paper, white
- plastic wrap
- scissors
- snack-sized candy bars (8–10), marbles (8–10), small foam spheres (8–10), or other objects to represent organisms
- other materials as requested by students

For each student
- safety goggles

SAFETY INFORMATION

Remind students to review all safety cautions and icons before beginning this lab.

PREPARATION

In this lab, students will explore ways that natural variation in a population can affect the survival of that population if the environment changes. Before you give each group its population of organisms, have the class work together to decide on an environment in which the organisms live. The environment should be relatively specific; if you wish, you may encourage students to choose a local area. Once students have received their populations, they should modify the members of each population slightly to produce variation in the population. Make sure the modifications are not too extreme; the "organisms" should still clearly be of the same "species," but with small natural variations. Students should assume that their population has lived in the area for a long time and so is well adapted to that area. For the directed-inquiry version of the lab, you will need to specify to students what niche or ecological role their organisms fill (e.g., top predator, decomposer, scavenger). For the guided-inquiry version, encourage students to be specific about the niche their population fills and the adaptations that help the organisms fill that niche.

Once students have created their populations, they will need to decide how the environment will change. Encourage them to choose a specific physical change (e.g., temperature or precipitation rate change, not a disease or an increase in predation). The class must agree on a specific type of change. Students must determine which members of their population (if any) would be able to survive in the new environment. Groups should share their results, paying special attention to justifying their assumptions and conclusions.

Skills Focus Applying Concepts, Making Predictions, Constructing Models

My Notes

_____

_____

_____

_____

_____

Exploration Lab continued

MODIFICATION FOR INDEPENDENT Inquiry

Have students conduct research on the effects of natural population variation on the survival of individual organisms and of the species as a whole. Students should identify testable questions relating to the concepts of natural variation and differential survival. They should design investigations, models, or controlled experiments to answer their questions. Allow students to carry out all reasonable procedures, and encourage them to share their findings with the class.

Answer Key for DIRECTED Inquiry

BUILD A MODEL

3. Answers will vary.

6. Sample answer: Our climate is very dry, so the organisms with the thickest skin will probably survive best because they will retain water best.

ANALYZE THE RESULTS

8. Sample answer: The organisms with thicker fur will probably have a hard time surviving in the new, warmer environment. Only two of our organisms have thin enough fur that they would probably be able to survive.

9. Answers will vary.

DRAW CONCLUSIONS

10. Sample answer: The more variability there was in the population, the more likely it was that at least one or two members of the population would survive the environmental change.

11. Sample answer: Populations that are very small probably have less variation than do larger populations. If a population has little variation, it is less likely to survive environmental changes or other changes, so it is more likely to become extinct.

Connect TO THE ESSENTIAL QUESTION

12. Sample answer: If the environment changes very dramatically and very quickly, it is less likely that organisms will be able to survive the change. Therefore, significant climate changes could cause many populations to die off at once.

Answer Key for GUIDED Inquiry

BUILD A MODEL

2. Answers will vary.

3. Answers will vary.

6. Sample answer: Our climate is very dry, so the organisms with the thickest skin will probably survive best because they will retain water best.

Exploration Lab continued

ANALYZE THE RESULTS

8. Sample answer: The organisms with thicker fur will probably have a hard time surviving in the new, warmer environment. Only two of our organisms have thin enough fur that they would probably be able to survive.

9. Answers will vary.

DRAW CONCLUSIONS

10. Sample answer: The more variability there was in the population, the more likely it was that at least one or two members of the population would survive the environmental change.

11. Sample answer: Populations that are very small probably have less variation than do larger populations. If a population has little variation, it is less likely to survive environmental changes or other changes, so it is more likely to become extinct.

Connect **TO THE ESSENTIAL QUESTION**

12. Sample answer: If the environment changes very dramatically and very quickly, it is less likely that organisms will be able to survive the change. Therefore, significant climate changes could cause many populations to die off at once.

EXPLORATION LAB DIRECTED *Inquiry*

Environmental Change and Evolution

In this lab, you will explore a model that illustrates how changes in the environment can affect the survival of organisms.

PROCEDURE

ASK A QUESTION

❶ In this lab, you will investigate the following question: How does variation within a population affect the survival of that population?

BUILD A MODEL

❷ Your teacher will give your group a group of **candy bars, marbles, or other objects.** These objects make up your population of "organisms." Your teacher will also describe to you what niche, or role, your organisms fill in the ecosystem.

❸ Identify some adaptations that your organisms have to their environment and niche. You will be able to modify your organisms slightly using the materials your teacher provides, so you can include those materials in your adaptations. For example, if your organisms live in a cold climate, you could say that one of their adaptations is that they are covered in cotton "fur." Record your ideas on a **separate sheet of paper.**

❹ Use **cotton balls, aluminum foil, plastic wrap, scissors, glue,** and **other materials** to modify your organisms as you described in Step 3. All of your organisms should look the same when you are done.

❺ Now you need to add variation to your population. All of the members of a given population are not identical. Each organism has slightly different characteristics than the others. Use additional materials to create variation in your population. For example, you might add extra cotton "fur" to one of your organisms. Remember that natural variations are generally small—for example, you should not modify one of your organisms so that it has wings if none of your other organisms has wings.

OBJECTIVE

- Model how natural variation in a population affects its survival.

MATERIALS

For each group

- aluminum foil
- cotton balls or batting
- feathers
- felt or cloth
- glue
- marker, permanent
- paper, white
- plastic wrap
- scissors
- objects to represent organisms (8–10)

For each student

- safety goggles

Exploration Lab continued

6 The variations between members of a population affect how well they survive and reproduce. Which of your organisms is most likely to survive and reproduce in the current environment? Explain your answer.

_____

_____

_____

_____

_____

7 Environments do not stay constant over time. As a class, decide on one specific way your organisms' environment will change. For example, the temperature might decrease by several degrees, or there might be more rainfall. Record the class's decision below.

_____

_____

_____

ANALYZE THE RESULTS

8 **Comparing Criteria** Which of your organisms, if any, will probably have a difficult time surviving in the new environment? How many members of your population do you think will survive the environmental change? Explain your answer.

_____

_____

_____

_____

_____

_____

_____

Exploration Lab continued

9 **Describing Results** Share your results with the rest of the class. In the space below, make notes about which groups' populations had the most and fewest survivors.

_____

_____

_____

_____

_____

_____

DRAW CONCLUSIONS

10 **Organizing Observations** How did the amount of variation in a population affect the fraction of that population that could survive the environmental change?

_____

_____

_____

_____

_____

_____

_____

_____

11 **Making Conclusions** Many populations, such as cheetahs and gorillas, have been greatly reduced in size by human actions. How might a small size make a population more susceptible to extinction?

_____

_____

_____

_____

_____

_____

_____

Name _____ Class _____ Date _____

Connect TO THE ESSENTIAL QUESTION

⑫ **Identifying Patterns** Many historical mass extinctions were accompanied by environmental changes. Use the results of this activity to explain how extreme environmental changes could cause mass extinctions.

_____

_____

_____

_____

_____

_____

_____

_____

_____

_____

Name _____ Class _____ Date _____

Environmental Change and Evolution

In this lab, you will explore a model that illustrates how changes in the environment can affect the survival of organisms.

PROCEDURE

1 In this lab, you will investigate the following question: How does variation within a population affect the survival of that population?

BUILD A MODEL

2 Your teacher will give your group a group of **candy bars, marbles, or other objects.** These objects make up your population of "organisms." Work with your group to decide what niche, or role, your organisms fill. For example, are they producers? Are they consumers? If they are consumers, are they predators, decomposers, scavengers, or something else? Record your group's decision below.

_____

_____

3 Identify some adaptations that your organisms have to their environment and niche. You will be able to modify your organisms slightly using the materials your teacher provides or other materials, so you can include those materials in your adaptations. For example, if your organisms live in a cold climate, you could say that one of their adaptations is that they are covered in cotton "fur." Record your ideas on a **separate sheet of paper.**

4 Use **assorted materials** to modify your organisms as you described in Step 3. If you need additional materials, ask your teacher for them. All of your organisms should look the same when you are done.

OBJECTIVE

- Model how natural variation in a population affects its survival.

MATERIALS

For each group
- aluminum foil
- cotton balls or batting
- feathers
- felt or cloth
- glue
- marker, permanent
- paper, white
- plastic wrap
- scissors
- objects to represent organisms (8–10)

For each student
- safety goggles

Exploration Lab continued

5 Now you need to add variation to your population. All of the members of a given population are not identical. Each organism has slightly different characteristics than the others. Use additional materials to create variation in your population. For example, you might add extra cotton "fur" to one of your organisms. Remember that natural variations are generally small—for example, you should not modify one of your organisms so that it has wings if none of your other organisms has wings.

6 The variations between members of a population affect how well they survive and reproduce. Which of your organisms is most likely to survive and reproduce in the current environment? Explain your answer.

_____

_____

_____

_____

_____

_____

7 Environments do not stay constant over time. As a class, decide on one specific way your organisms' environment will change. For example, the temperature might decrease by several degrees, or there might be more rainfall. Record the class's decision below.

_____

_____

_____

Name _____ Class _____ Date _____

ANALYZE THE RESULTS

8 **Comparing Criteria** Which of your organisms, if any, will probably have a difficult time surviving in the new environment? How many members of your population do you think will survive the environmental change? Explain your answer.

_____

_____

_____

_____

_____

_____

9 **Describing Results** Share your results with the rest of the class. In the space below, make notes about which groups' populations had the most and fewest survivors.

_____

_____

_____

_____

_____

_____

Exploration Lab continued

DRAW CONCLUSIONS

10 **Organizing Observations** How did the amount of variation in a population affect the fraction of that population that could survive the environmental change?

_____

_____

_____

_____

_____

_____

11 **Making Conclusions** Many populations, such as cheetahs and gorillas, have been greatly reduced in size by human actions. How might a small size make a population more susceptible to extinction?

_____

_____

_____

_____

Connect TO THE ESSENTIAL QUESTION

12 **Identifying Patterns** Many historical mass extinctions were accompanied by environmental changes. Use the results of this activity to explain how extreme environmental changes could cause mass extinctions.

_____

_____

_____

_____

_____

_____

_____

_____

_____

_____

QUICK LAB DIRECTED *Inquiry*

Comparing Anatomy GENERAL

👥 Small groups
🕐 15 minutes

LAB RATINGS

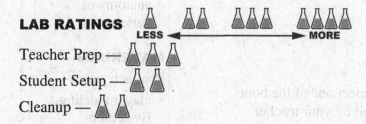

Teacher Prep —

Student Setup —

Cleanup —

MATERIALS

For each group

• clay, modeling, five colors

• colored pencils, five colors

• picture of animal anatomy

SAFETY INFORMATION

Remind students to review all safety cautions and icons before beginning this lab.

Make sure that students do not have allergies to clay.

Remind students to never eat or taste anything in the lab.

My Notes

_____

_____

_____

_____

_____

TEACHER NOTES

In this activity, students will compare the anatomy of several vertebrates. Provide students with pictures of animal anatomies. There are many books and websites that provide high-quality images perfect for this activity.

   If time permits, allow students to research pictures of animal anatomies and choose their own picture to work from.

Skills Focus Making Models, Comparing Results

MODIFICATION FOR INDEPENDENT *Inquiry*

Direct students to research the anatomy of two specific, but different, species. Students will create models to compare and contrast the two anatomies. Students can present their completed models to the class. Models can be drawings, computer generated, or 3-dimensional sculptures.

Answer Key

4. Sample answer: Bats have long, thin finger bones that support the skin that forms the wings.

QUICK LAB DIRECTED Inquiry

QUICK LAB DIRECTED Inquiry

Comparing Anatomy

In this lab, you will compare the anatomy of several vertebrate animals. You will create a model of a selected vertebrate that you will present to the class, then compare your model to the models of other groups.

PROCEDURE

❶ Each member of the group should select one of the bone arrangements in the **picture** provided by your teacher.

❷ In the space below, draw an outline of your selected animal's limb.

OBJECTIVE

- Compare the anatomy of vertebrates.

MATERIALS

For each group

- clay, modeling, five colors
- colored pencils, five colors
- picture of animal anatomy

❸ Shape **modeling clay** into the limb bones. Position the model bones within the outline. If possible, use colors that are consistent with the illustration. Otherwise, decide as a group which colors will be used for specific bones. Record your decisions below.

_____

_____

_____

Quick Lab continued

4 Look at the models created by other groups. Compare the shape of each bone as it appears in different limbs. Discuss how the size and shape of each bone relates to its function.

_____

_____

_____

_____

_____

_____

_____

_____

_____

QUICK LAB **DIRECTED** Inquiry

Genetic Evidence for Evolution GENERAL

👥 Individual student
🕐 30 minutes

LAB RATINGS

LESS ←——————→ MORE

Teacher Prep —
Student Setup —
Cleanup —

SAFETY INFORMATION

Remind students to review all safety cautions before beginning this lab.

TEACHER NOTES

In this activity, the student is challenged to compare DNA from several species and to derive an evolutionary tree based on their characteristics. The more closely related two organisms are, the greater the similarity in their DNA. The teacher will explain that DNA can therefore be used to infer species relatedness. Using the sequences, the student will draw an evolutionary tree (cladogram). The cladogram will include the differences in the genetic sequences on the tree.

Tip This activity may help students understand that species relatedness can be determined by examination of DNA sequences.

Student Tip Start with the species that share the most DNA bases and work your way back.

Skills Focus Devising Procedures, Drawing Conclusions

MODIFICATION FOR GUIDED Inquiry

Have students develop the method to establish relatedness rather than having them follow directions for using the DNA sequences.

MATERIALS

For each student
• paper
• pencil

My Notes

_____
_____
_____
_____
_____

Answer Key

1. Sample answer: The bases in the DNA sequence are almost identical. This means that they code for the same gene.

3. There are two correct answers to this question. Pair A and B are identical in sequence as are pair D and E. Because two species share the same sequence they are more closely related than two species that show differences in gene sequence.

4. Students should have both A and B as a closely related pair and also D and E as a closely related pair in their collective answers to Questions 3 and 4.

5. See the phylogenetic tree diagram below:

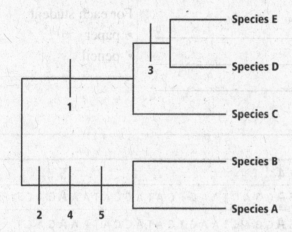

Genetic Evidence for Evolution

In this lab, you will investigate a method for using DNA to infer how species are related. Using the DNA sequences provided, you will draw an evolutionary tree showing the relationships between several organisms.

PROCEDURE

❶ The table below shows one section of the same gene found in five different organisms. The organisms are labeled A, B, C, D, and E. What clue shows that this DNA is from the same gene in all of these organisms? Explain.

_____

_____

_____

OBJECTIVE

• Use similarities and differences in DNA sequences to determine the evolutionary relationships between several organisms.

MATERIALS

For each student
• paper
• pencil

A COMPARISON OF DNA SEQUENCES

Species	Sites of differences in genetic sequences
	1 **2** **3** **4** **5**
Species A	A C C A G C **C** T G T G C A A C G A T G **A** C G A C T A A G T G A T A C C A T A A **A** G A C T
Species B	A C C A G C **C** T G T G C A A C G A T G **A** C G A C T A A G T G A T A C C A T A A **A** G A C T
Species C	A C **G** A G C T T G T G C A A C G A T G C C G A C T A A G T G A T A C C A T A A C G A C T
Species D	A C **G** A G C T T G T G C A **T** C G A T G C C G A C T A A G T G A T A C C A T A A C G A C T
Species E	A C **G** A G C T T G T G C A **T** C G A T G C C G A C T A A G T G A T A C C A T A A C G A C T

❷ Circle all of the places on the table where you think changes have taken place as a result of evolution.

❸ Based on the changes you noted, name one pair of organisms that are very closely related to one another. Explain why you think so.

_____

_____

❹ Now name another pair of organisms that are also very closely related to one another.

_____

_____

Quick Lab continued

❺ Use the information about genetic relatedness to try to sort the five
organisms into positions on the phylogenetic tree shown below. Place the
capital letter corresponding to each species next to one of the branches on
the far right of the tree.

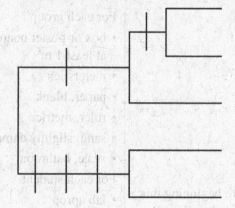

FIELD LAB `DIRECTED Inquiry` **OR** `GUIDED Inquiry`

Mystery Footprints `GENERAL`

🧑‍🤝‍🧑 Small groups
🕐 90 minutes

LAB RATINGS

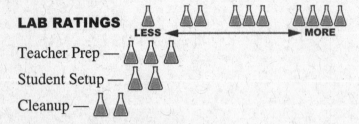

LESS ← → MORE

Teacher Prep —

Student Setup —

Cleanup —

MATERIALS

For each group
- box or poster board, at least 1 m^2
- meterstick
- paper, blank
- ruler, metric
- sand, slightly damp
- scale, bathroom

For each student
- lab apron
- safety goggles

SAFETY INFORMATION

Remind students to review all safety cautions and icons before beginning this lab. Provide students with ample space and a safe location to test walking and running on the sandy area. Remind each group of students to keep out of the way of others. Have students keep shoes, or at least socks, on unless they are actively making footprints. Caution students that spilled sand can be a slipping hazard, and all spills should be reported and cleaned up immediately.

My Notes
_____
_____
_____
_____
_____

TEACHER NOTES

In this activity, students will investigate a set of mystery footprints and study their own footprints in order to infer information about the person or persons who made the mystery prints. Explain to students that a scientist should be able to make the same type of inferences about an organism from fresh tracks as from preserved tracks. Emphasize that although in this lab they will be looking at preserved tracks in sand, the same techniques that they use can be applied to the study of fossilized tracks. Students will then gather and organize data and look for trends and patterns to support their inferences regarding the mystery prints.

To set up this lab, you will need to either find a sandy area outside or construct a long, shallow sandbox out of wood or cardboard. You may prefer to perform this activity outside because it is likely to be messy. Before class, ask a boy and a girl (preferably students who are not in your science class) or two adults, one male and one female, to walk through the sand in their bare feet. The sand should be about 16 cm deep, and the area to be walked through should be long enough that three or four footprints can be seen in the sand. Slightly moistened sand will hold the best footprints. You may want to make the footprints more permanent by using plaster of Paris. If you do not have access to sand, look for a type of soil that will hold a footprint.

If resources are limited, you may choose to make this an activity that the entire class can do together as a large group. Instead of having all the groups create their own footprints, simply have a few student volunteers make footprints that the entire class can analyze. You may also consider this modification if there are students who would not be comfortable being weighed in front of their classmates.

Field Lab continued

Tip This activity may help students understand how scientists use fossil evidence to follow the evolution of a species.

Student Tip Try to have people of very different sizes make the footprints so that you can get as much information from your models as possible.

Skills Focus Constructing Models, Examining Evidence, Drawing Conclusions

MODIFICATION FOR INDEPENDENT Inquiry

Show students photographs of trace fossils. Ask them what kind of information they think scientists can infer from trace fossils. Challenge students to create "trace fossils" of several similar items and compare and contrast the impressions that each item makes. Use students' results to begin a discussion of the uses and limitations of trace fossils in the study of evolution.

Answer Key for DIRECTED Inquiry

ASK A QUESTION

1. Sample answer: What can we tell about people just based on the footprints they made?

MAKE OBSERVATIONS

2. Answers will vary.

DEVELOP A PLAN

3. Sample answer: We could tell its height and weight, how it walked, whether it was running or walking, if it was alone or part of a group, and what kind of environment it lived in.

4. Answers will vary.

MAKE OBSERVATIONS

6. Answers will vary.

ANALYZE THE RESULTS

7. Answers will vary.

8. Sample answer: I think two different people made the footprints because there seems to be a track of one large set of prints, and then another track next to it of slightly smaller prints. The prints within each set are consistent in size, depth, and stride.

DRAW CONCLUSIONS

9. Answers will vary.

10. Sample answer: We can't tell for sure how old the people were or if they were male or female. For example, a young boy might make the same size tracks as a small woman. We also can't tell if the different tracks were made at the same time by people walking together, or if they were made at different times by different people walking in the same area.

Connect TO THE ESSENTIAL QUESTION

11. Sample answer: They could see if the size or depth of the footprints changed over time, because that would show that the body type of the species had changed.

Answer Key for GUIDED Inquiry

ASK A QUESTION

1. Sample answer: What can we tell about people just based on the footprints they made?

MAKE OBSERVATIONS

2. Answers will vary.

DEVELOP A PLAN

3. Sample answer: We could tell its height and weight, how it walked, whether it was running or walking, if it was alone or part of a group, and what kind of environment it lived in.

4. Sample answer: It will help because it will give us something to compare the mystery footprints to. For example, if one of us weighs 150 lb and makes footprints that are deeper than the mystery footprints, then we can say that the person who made the mystery footprints probably weighed less than 150 lb.

5. Answers will vary.

BUILD A MODEL

6. Answers will vary.

MAKE OBSERVATIONS

8. Answers will vary.

ANALYZE THE RESULTS

9. Answers will vary.

10. Sample answer: I think two different people made the footprints because there seems to be a track of one large set of prints, and then another track next to it of slightly smaller prints. The prints within each set are consistent in size, depth, and stride.

DRAW CONCLUSIONS

11. Answers will vary.

12. Sample answer: We can't tell for sure how old the people were or if they were male or female. For example, a young boy might make the same size tracks as a small woman. We also can't tell if the different tracks were made at the same time by people walking together, or if they were made at different times by different people walking in the same area.

Connect TO THE ESSENTIAL QUESTION

13. Sample answer: They could see if the size or depth of the footprints changed over time because that would show that the body type of the species had changed.

FIELD LAB DIRECTED *Inquiry*

Mystery Footprints

In this lab, you will explore a set of footprints left by a person or persons unknown. You will create your own model footprints to help you infer information about the person or persons who made the mystery footprints.

PROCEDURE

ASK A QUESTION

❶ Your teacher will show you some mystery footprints in sand. Examine the mystery footprints. Brainstorm what you might learn about the people who walked on this patch of sand. Write your experimental question in the space provided.

_____

_____

MAKE OBSERVATIONS

❷ Examine the mystery footprints. Use a **ruler** to measure the dimensions of the footprints. Record your data in the table below.

MYSTERY FOOTPRINTS

	Footprint set 1	Footprint set 2
Length		
Width		
Depth of toe		
Depth of heel		
Length of stride		

OBJECTIVES

• Compare model footprints to the footprints of unknown people.
• Describe features of unknown people based on their footprints.

MATERIALS

For each group
• box or poster board, at least 1 m²
• meterstick
• paper, blank
• ruler, metric
• sand, slightly damp
• scale, bathroom
For each student
• lab apron
• safety goggles

Field Lab continued

DEVELOP A PLAN

❸ Discuss as a group what type of information you can infer about an animal from its footprint. List some of your ideas.

_____

_____

_____

_____

_____

_____

❹ On a separate **sheet of paper**, create a table for the data you will collect. Include the height and weight of each person making the footprints. You should also include space to describe each person's activity type, as well as spaces for any characteristics you will measure. Decide who will create the footprints and what activity they will perform.

BUILD A MODEL

❺ Use the **sand** provided to create your own model footprints in a **box** or on **poster board**. This will make it possible for you to test how different factors such as activity type (e.g., running or walking) and body type (e.g., height and weight) affect the appearance of footprints.

MAKE OBSERVATIONS

❻ Examine the model footprints your group has made, and record your observations in your table. Sketch them in the space below.

Field Lab continued

ANALYZE THE RESULTS

7 **Classifying Data** Compare the data from your footprints with the data from the mystery footprints. How are the footprints alike? How are they different?

_____

_____

_____

_____

_____

_____

_____

8 **Identifying Patterns** How many people do you think made the mystery footprints? Explain your interpretation.

_____

_____

_____

_____

_____

DRAW CONCLUSIONS

9 **Interpreting Results** Can you tell if the mystery footprints were made by men, women, children, or a combination? Can you tell if they were standing still, walking, or running? Explain your interpretation.

_____

_____

_____

_____

_____

Field Lab continued

10 Evaluating Models What are the limitations of your model footprints?
Is there information you cannot get from the footprints?

_____
_____
_____
_____
_____
_____
_____
_____
_____

Connect TO THE ESSENTIAL QUESTION

11 Applying Concepts Trace fossils are impressions made in substrate by the
movements of organisms. Fossil footprints are an example of a type of trace
fossil that scientists use to gather information about ancient species. Describe
an example of how trace fossils might show how a modern species has evolved
over time.

_____
_____
_____
_____
_____
_____
_____
_____
_____
_____
_____
_____

FIELD LAB GUIDED *Inquiry*

Mystery Footprints

In this lab, you will explore a set of footprints left by a person or persons unknown. You will create your own model footprints to help you infer information about the person or persons who made the mystery footprints.

PROCEDURE

ASK A QUESTION

1 Your teacher will show you some mystery footprints in sand. Examine the mystery footprints. Brainstorm what you might learn about the people who walked on this patch of sand. Write your experimental question in the space provided.

_____

_____

_____

_____

MAKE OBSERVATIONS

2 Examine the mystery footprints. What types of features can you measure? How would you measure them? Make the measurements and record your results in a data table.

DEVELOP A PLAN

3 Discuss as a group what type of information you can infer about an animal from its footprint. List some of your ideas.

_____

_____

_____

_____

_____

OBJECTIVES

- Compare model footprints to the footprints of unknown people.
- Describe features of unknown people based on their footprints.

MATERIALS

For each group
- box or poster board, at least 1 m^2
- meterstick
- paper, blank
- ruler, metric
- sand, slightly damp
- scale, bathroom

For each student
- lab apron
- safety goggles

Field Lab continued

❹ How can making your own model footprints help you to infer information about the people who made the mystery footprints?

_____

_____

_____

_____

❺ Describe how you will make your model footprints using a **box** or **poster board** and the **sand** that your teacher provided. How many footprints will you make? How will each set of footprints differ from the others? What will you measure on each set of footprints?

_____

_____

_____

_____

_____

_____

_____

_____

_____

_____

_____

BUILD A MODEL

❻ On a **separate piece of paper**, create a data table that will help you to organize the information you collect about your model footprints.

❼ Once your teacher has approved your plans, create your model footprints.

MAKE OBSERVATIONS

❽ Examine the model footprints your group has made, and record your observations in your data table.

Field Lab continued

ANALYZE THE RESULTS

9 **Classifying Data** Compare the data from your footprints with the data from the mystery footprints. How are the footprints alike? How are they different?

_____
_____
_____
_____
_____
_____
_____

10 **Identifying Patterns** How many people do you think made the mystery footprints? Explain your interpretation.

_____
_____
_____
_____
_____
_____
_____
_____

DRAW CONCLUSIONS

11 **Interpreting Results** Can you tell if the mystery footprints were made by men, women, children, or a combination? Can you tell if they were standing still, walking, or running? Explain your interpretation.

_____
_____
_____
_____
_____
_____
_____
_____

Field Lab continued

⑫ Evaluating Models What are the limitations of your model footprints?
Is there information you cannot get from the footprints?

_____

_____

_____

_____

_____

Connect TO THE ESSENTIAL QUESTION

⑬ Applying Concepts Trace fossils are impressions made in substrate by the
movements of organisms. Fossil footprints are an example of a type of trace
fossil that scientists use to gather information about ancient species. Describe
an example of how trace fossils might show how a modern species has evolved
over time.

_____

_____

_____

_____

_____

How Do We Know What Happened When? GENERAL

👥 Individual student
🕑 30 minutes

LAB RATINGS

LESS ◄————————► MORE

Teacher Prep —

Student Setup —

Cleanup —

MATERIALS
For each student
• index cards
• string
• tape

My Notes

_____

_____

_____

_____

_____

TEACHER NOTES

In this activity, students use personal life histories to distinguish between the implications of minor versus major events in creating a timeline. This is analogous to how paleontologists use index fossils to create evidence-based geologic timelines. Students may have a difficult time making the conceptual transition from their personal life story to the geological timeline. It is worthwhile to ensure that students understand this connection before wrapping up the activity.

Skills Focus Making Models, Applying Concepts

MODIFICATION FOR INDEPENDENT Inquiry

Some types of data prove to be more important than others in enabling conclusions based on evidence to be drawn. Have students consider the following questions after they complete the personal history activity:

• Have living things changed over the course of Earth's long history?
• Are all related animals both similar and different?
• Do some living things today look different from their ancient relatives?
• Can some things that once existed on Earth no longer be found?
• Does life on Earth continue to change today?
• What can you discover by observing fossils?

Have students conduct independent research inspired by one of these questions and then formulate a reasonable explanation based on their research. Students' reports should incorporate at least two of the following:

Quick Lab continued

- Specific quantitative and qualitative data that supports the proposed explanation
- Specific quantitative and qualitative data that supports observed patterns and relationships
- An evaluation of the reasonableness of the proposed explanation
- An analysis of whether evidence supports the proposed explanation

Answer Key

5. Sample answer: Commonplace events, such as eating breakfast, are not suitable for developing a timeline that covers a longer time period. Although important, they are repetitive and trivial.

6. Sample answer: Special events, for example, when a person is born or marries, provide unique markers for developing a timeline.

7. Sample answer: commonplace and recurring versus rare and unique.

8. Answers may vary.

9. Index fossils are unique to a particular rock layer and, thus, to a particular time period. Fossils in lower rock layers are older than fossils in upper rock layers. This geologic evidence can be used to provide information about the history of life on Earth.

10. For an individual, an index event is rare and highly characteristic of a particular time period.

How Do We Know What Happened When?

When you think of it, every person's life story is a history of minor and major events. Some events, like the day you found a $5 dollar bill, are trivial and will soon be forgotten. Others, such as the family's trip to the mountains, are memories that will forever remain. In this lab, you will use your personal life history to create a timeline that highlights major events in your life.

PROCEDURE

❶ Put your name on the blank line in the top of the first column in the table below. In the Events column, enter 15–20 events that have occurred in your life. Don't do a lot of thinking, just include things that immediately come to mind.

❷ In the Date column, enter the date or dates when these events happened.

OBJECTIVES
- Create a timeline highlighting major life events.
- Describe how fossils can be used to construct geologic timelines.

MATERIALS
For each student
- index cards
- string
- tape

SIGNIFICANT LIFE EVENTS

Events in the life of _____	Date when it happened	Events in the life of _____	Date when It happened

❸ Compare your list with your lab partner's list. Discuss the similarities and differences. Did you overlook any significant events?

❹ Write each event on a separate **index card.** Arrange the index cards in order from oldest to most recent and use **tape** to attach them to the **string.** You have created a timeline.

Quick Lab continued

5 Are there any events in your personal timeline that are difficult to arrange in the order in which they happened? If yes, what are they, and why isn't it easy for them to be arranged that way?

_____

_____

6 Are there any events in your personal timeline that are simple to arrange in the proper order? If yes, what are they, and why is it easy for them to be sequenced?

_____

_____

7 What is the general difference between the events you identified in Questions 5 and 6?

_____

_____

8 Is there anything about certain events that makes them better than others at telling your life story? If so, what makes these events special?

_____

_____

9 Paleontologists are scientists who use fossil evidence to create a "story" about the history of life on Earth. Some fossils are found in many different rock layers. Other fossils occur only in certain rock layers. These fossils are called "index fossils." What makes index fossils so important to paleontologists?

_____

_____

10 How are index fossils like the special events in your own life history? What are the characteristics of special "index events" that can be used to describe a person's life?

_____

_____

QUICK LAB GUIDED Inquiry

QUICK LAB GUIDED Inquiry

Investigate Relative and Absolute Age GENERAL

👥 Small groups
🕐 20 minutes

LAB RATINGS

LESS ◄———————————► MORE

Teacher Prep —

Student Setup —

Cleanup —

TEACHER NOTES

In this activity, students will use a model to investigate relative and absolute age. Collect newspapers over a period of several weeks leading up to this activity, or ask each student to bring in one or two newspapers from different days. Tape each pencil to an undated newspaper, and point out that each newspaper represents a separate layer of rock and that those with pencils represent layers that contain a fossil.

Tip This activity will help students better understand the difference between *relative* and *absolute*. Students most likely understand the definition of absolute but may not understand that relative refers to the relationship between two things. Relatives in our families are connected in a particular way. Review the definition of both words with students prior to beginning this activity.

Student Tip How can you tell someone's approximate age? How can you tell their absolute age? How can you explore this scenario with rocks instead of people?

Skills Focus Making Models, Making Inferences

MODIFICATION FOR DIRECTED Inquiry

Prepare the model yourself and complete the activity as a class. As the students examine the pencils between the newspaper layers, ask students to identify which pencil is oldest and which is youngest. Then have students put all the pencils in order by their relative ages. Next, ask students how they can use the dates on the newspaper to narrow down the age of the pencils. Ask, *Is this an example of absolute dating or relative dating?* Students should recognize that although they can narrow down the age of the pencils to between two dates, they still do not know the absolute date.

MODIFICATION FOR INDEPENDENT Inquiry

Give groups the materials and ask them how they can use newspapers and pencils to model relative and absolute aging in rocks. Have students present their plans to you for approval and allow them to carry out all approved plans.

MATERIALS

For each group
• newspapers with different dates (5)
• pencils (2)

My Notes

_____

_____

_____

_____

_____

Quick Lab continued

Answer Key

2. The pencils represent fossils found between layers of rock.

3. Sample answer: The pencil at the bottom of the stack has been there longest.

4. Sample answer: This is similar to finding the relative age of rocks and fossils because the rocks and fossils found in the lower layers of rock are the older ones.

5. Now I can give a closer estimate of when the pencil was buried in the stack of newspapers. I know that it happened sometime between two specific dates.
Teacher Prompt Is there any way to tell the absolute age of the pencil? (No.) What does knowing the dates of the newspapers help you do? (Narrow down the age of the pencils.)

6. Sample answer: This is different from finding the absolute age of rocks and fossils because we are not running tests on the rocks and fossils themselves in order to learn their age. We are only inferring that one fossil is older than another by their relative positions in layers of rock.

7. Before looking at the dates, you could only tell the relative "age" of the pencils by their positions in the stack of newspapers. After looking at the dates, you could tell more specifically, using dates or days, when the pencils were placed on the newspapers.
Teacher Prompt Point out to students that although you have a better idea as to when the pencils were placed on the stack, you still cannot tell the absolute age of the pencils.

QUICK LAB GUIDED *Inquiry*

Investigate Relative and Absolute Age

In this activity, you will use newspapers to model rock layers and pencils to model fossils in the rock. You will use your model to make inferences about relative and absolute age.

PROCEDURE

1 Have one person in your group arrange the newspapers in a pile with the oldest newspaper on the bottom and the newest on top.

2 After the newspapers are stacked, tape each pencil to an undated newspaper. How do the pencils represent fossils?

_____

_____

3 Imagine that the newspapers were really placed on the stack on the days they were published, sometimes on top of a pencil and sometimes not. None of the papers or pencils were moved again, however. Which pencil has probably been there longest?

_____

4 How is this model similar to rocks and fossils found in Earth's crust?

_____

_____

_____

_____

5 Look at the dates on the newspapers. What do the dates tell you about the pencils in the stack?

_____

_____

_____

OBJECTIVES

- Create a model of rock layers that contain fossils.
- Investigate the difference between relative and absolute age.

MATERIALS

For each group
- newspapers with different dates (5)
- pencils (2)

Quick Lab continued

6 How is this different from finding the absolute age of rocks and fossils?

_____

_____

_____

7 How does the information you collected about the "ages" of the pencils before looking at the newspaper dates differ from what you collected after looking at the dates?

_____

_____

_____

QUICK LAB DIRECTED Inquiry

Using a Dichotomous Key GENERAL

👤 Individual student
🕐 10 minutes

MATERIALS

For each student
• pencil

LAB RATINGS

LESS ◀——————▶ MORE

Teacher Prep —

Student Setup —

Cleanup —

My Notes

_____

_____

_____

_____

_____

SAFETY INFORMATION

Remind students to review all safety cautions and icons before beginning this lab.

TEACHER NOTES

Dichotomous keys are used to identify living things based on observable characteristics. Dichotomous keys for plants are very common. Students might benefit from seeing dichotomous keys in commercially published field guides as they begin this activity. In this activity, students will use a dichotomous key to help identify an organism. Then they will modify the dichotomous key to identify another animal.

Skills Focus Drawing Conclusions, Developing Methods

MODIFICATION FOR GUIDED Inquiry

Instead of giving students the dichotomous key for identifying the long-tailed weasel, have students create their own dichotomous keys for an organism of their choice. They should choose an organism and create a dichotomous key that will identify that organism. Keys should be organized according to the physical characteristics of the organism and should include at least five steps.

Answer Key

1. Sample answer: long-tailed weasel

2. Sample answer: Ask which mammal has white feet and which mammal has brown fur.
   Teacher Prompt Ask students what characteristics they can think of that would be used to distinguish between a white-footed mouse and a brown field rat.

3. Sample answer:

5.	a.	This mammal has a long, furry tail that is black on the tip.	long-tailed weasel
	b.	This mammal has a long tail that has little fur.	Go to Step 6.

4. Sample answer:

6.	a.	This mammal has white feet.	white-footed mouse
	b.	This mammal has brown fur.	brown field rat

Using a Dichotomous Key

In this lab, you will use a dichotomous key to identify an organism. Then you will modify the dichotomous key to identify another organism.

PROCEDURE

1 Use the dichotomous key shown below to identify an organism that has a furry tail with a black tip and no mask. According to the key, what is the organism?

_____

_____

_____

OBJECTIVE
• Use a dichotomous key to identify an organism.
MATERIALS
For each student
• pencil

DICHOTOMOUS KEY TO SIX COMMON MAMMALS IN THE EASTERN UNITED STATES

1. a. This mammal has no hair on its tail. b. This mammal has hair on its tail.	Go to Step 2. Go to Step 3.
2. a. This mammal has a short, naked tail. b. This mammal has a long, naked tail.	eastern mole Go to Step 4.
3. a. This mammal has a black mask across its face. b. This mammal does not have a black mask across its face.	raccoon Go to Step 5.
4. a. This mammal has a tail that is flat and paddle shaped. b. This mammal has a tail that is not flat or paddle shaped.	beaver opossum
5. a. This mammal has a long, furry tail that is black on the tip. b. This mammal has a long tail that has little fur.	longtail weasel white-footed mouse

Quick Lab continued

❷ Both the white-footed mouse and the brown field rat have long tails with little fur. How could you modify Step 5 to help identify the mouse and the rat?

_____

_____

_____

_____

❸ Write the modified version of Step 5 in the table below.

5. a.	
b.	

❹ What additional step would you need to identify the mouse and the rat? Write your answer in the table below.

6. a.	
b.	

Quick Lab continued

QUICK LAB DIRECTED *Inquiry*

Investigate Classifying Leaves GENERAL

👥 Small groups
🕐 20 minutes

LAB RATINGS

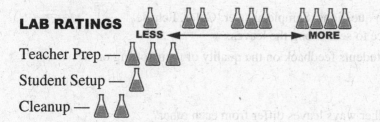

LESS ◄———————► MORE

Teacher Prep —

Student Setup —

Cleanup —

MATERIALS

For each group
• leaves, various
• magnifying lens

My Notes

_____
_____
_____
_____
_____
_____

SAFETY INFORMATION

Remind students to review all safty cautions and the icon before beginning
this lab.

TEACHER NOTES

In this activity, students will decide on a classification scheme for leaves.
Begin by telling students: "The question for this lab is, 'How can we classify
a set of tree leaves?' Use your student datasheet to guide your thinking."
Students will then observe a collection of leaves and then use their systems to classify
leaves into groups.

Tip If leaves are not available, you may need to use pictures of leaves from books,
magazines, or online sources.

Skills Focus Observing Characteristics, Classifying Materials

MODIFICATION FOR GUIDED *Inquiry*

As a Guided Inquiry, you can provide students with the challenge of classifying the leaves
using two different characteristics without the support of the questions on the Directed
Inquiry Student Datasheet. Allow students to sort and then ask them to compare the results
and to examine the success of the classification system.

Answer Key

1. Accept all reasonable answers. Sample answer: color, length, width, smooth edges, jagged edges.
   Teacher Prompt What kinds of characteristics make the leaves different from each other?

2. Accept all reasonable answers for both questions. Sample answer: Color. I chose color because it is the easiest difference to see among the leaves.

3. Accept all reasonable answers. Give students feedback on the quality of their sorting or if you notice inconsistencies.

4. Accept all reasonable answers.
   Teacher Prompt What are some other ways leaves differ from each other?

5. Accept all reasonable answers.

Investigate Classifying Leaves

In this lab, you will apply your understanding of characteristics and classification to develop a system for classifying a variety of leaves. You will use two different classification systems to sort the leaves and then compare the results of the two sorts.

OBJECTIVE
• Develop a classification scheme for tree leaves.

MATERIALS
For each group
• leaves, various
• magnifying lens

PROCEDURE

1 Scientists use classification systems to understand the natural world. Today, you will have a chance to develop your own classification system for tree leaves. Brainstorm some characteristics of leaves that might be useful in categorizing them.

_____

_____

2 Which of the characteristics listed above will you use to classify the leaves? Why did you pick this characteristic?

_____

3 Use your characteristic to sort the set of tree leaves into groups. Use the space below to describe the resulting groups of leaves.

_____

_____

_____

_____

Quick Lab continued

④ Pick a different characteristic and sort the leaves into new groups. How are the resulting groups similar and/or different than the initial groups you created?

_____

_____

⑤ A student says, "The best way to sort tree leaves is by size." Do you agree? Explain your answer.

_____

_____

_____

EXPLORATION LAB [DIRECTED Inquiry] OR [GUIDED Inquiry]

Developing Scientific Names [GENERAL]

👥 Individual student
🕐 45 minutes

LAB RATINGS

LESS ◀——————————▶ MORE

Teacher Prep —

Student Setup —

Cleanup —

MATERIALS

For each student
- chart of Latin and Greek terms
- paper, blank (2 sheets)

My Notes

_____
_____
_____
_____
_____

TEACHER NOTES

In this activity, students will practice using Greek and Latin word roots to develop two-part scientific names for imaginary organisms. This lab will help students demonstrate an understanding of binomial nomenclature by using a key to assign scientific names to fictional organisms. After completing the lab, students should be able to explain the function of the scientific naming system. You will need to provide students with a list of Greek and Latin prefixes, suffixes, and roots commonly used in scientific names. Remind students that the genus name is capitalized but the species name is not and that both words must be underlined or italicized.

Tip This lab may help students understand the use of binomial nomenclature in taxonomy.

Student Tip Try to make your names as descriptive and specific as possible.

Skills Focus Making Observations, Analyzing Criteria

MODIFICATION FOR [INDEPENDENT Inquiry]

Have students design fictional animals. They should draw their animals and write a brief description of the animals' habitat, diet, and any other information they wish to include. Collect and redistribute the animals, and challenge each student to create a scientific name for his or her assigned animal. You may wish to have students present their assigned animals to the class and explain how they chose their names.

Answer Key for [DIRECTED Inquiry]

MAKE OBSERVATIONS

3. Answers will vary.

4. Answers will vary.

ANALYZE THE RESULTS

5. Answers will vary.

6. Sample answer: They all have two eyes.

DRAW CONCLUSIONS

7. They can use the two parts to organize animals into related groups. For example, closely related animals could all share the first name, and then each animal could have a unique second name to set it apart from the rest of the group.

Connect TO THE ESSENTIAL QUESTION

8. Sample answer: no, because that name applies to more than one organism.

Answer Key for GUIDED Inquiry

DEVELOP A PLAN

2. Sample answer: body shape, size, number of feet, number of antennae, whether they have a mouth, whether they have a tail.

EVALUATE THE PLAN

3. Answers will vary.

4. Sample answer: yes.

6. Answers will vary.

ANALYZE THE RESULTS

7. Sample answer: They all have two eyes.

DRAW CONCLUSIONS

8. They can use the two parts to organize animals into related groups. For example, closely related animals could all share the first name, and then each animal could have a unique second name to set it apart from the rest of the group.

Connect TO THE ESSENTIAL QUESTION

9. Sample answer: no, because that name applies to more than one organism.

EXPLORATION LAB DIRECTED Inquiry

Developing Scientific Names

In this lab, you will use Greek and Latin terms to create descriptive and unique two-part scientific names for fictional organisms.

PROCEDURE

MAKE OBSERVATIONS

❶ Carefully examine the fictional organisms pictured below. Think about what features they all have in common and what makes each organism unique.

OBJECTIVE
• Create scientific names to describe fictional organisms.

MATERIALS
For each student
• chart of Latin and Greek terms
• paper, blank (2 sheets)

❷ On a **separate sheet of paper**, make a chart like the one shown below. Include one row for each organism.

Organism #	Shape	Size	Other features	Scientific name

❸ Describe the features of each organism. Record your observations in your chart. An example for the second organism is shown below.

Organism #	Shape	Size	Other features	Scientific name
2	circle	medium	4 antennae	

Exploration Lab continued

4 Use your **list of Latin and Greek terms** to create scientific names for each organism. The first name should describe the organism's general body type, and the second name should be more specific and describe any combination of features. Record your names in your chart. An example for the second organism is shown below.

Organism #	Shape	Size	Other features	Scientific name
2	circle	medium	4 antennae	*Cyclomorph quadantennae*

ANALYZE THE RESULTS

5 **Evaluating Methods** Were you able to think of a unique name for each organism? Which animals were the most difficult to name, and why?

_____

_____

_____

_____

_____

_____

_____

_____

_____

6 **Organizing Data** Name a characteristic that all of your organisms share.

_____

_____

Exploration Lab continued

DRAW CONCLUSIONS

7 **Identifying Costs and Benefits** Scientific names have two parts, even though it would be easy to give each species one long name. Can you think of how scientists might use two-part names when studying how different species are related?

_____

_____

_____

_____

_____

_____

_____

_____

_____

_____

_____

_____

_____

_____

_____

Connect TO THE ESSENTIAL QUESTION

8 **Evaluating Results** If you gave species 1 a common name, such as *round-face-no-nose*, would any other scientist know which of the organisms you were referring to? Explain your answer.

_____

_____

_____

_____

_____

_____

_____

EXPLORATION LAB GUIDED (Inquiry)

Developing Scientific Names

In this lab, you will use Greek and Latin terms to create descriptive
and unique two-part scientific names for fictional organisms.

PROCEDURE

MAKE OBSERVATIONS

❶ Carefully examine the fictional organisms pictured below.
Think about what features they all have in common and what
makes each organism unique.

OBJECTIVE
- Create scientific
  names to describe
  fictional organisms.

MATERIALS
For each student
- chart of Latin and
  Greek terms
- paper, blank
  (2 sheets)

DEVELOP A PLAN

❷ Scientists often name new species according to how they look. Using names
that describe several different features helps to make the name unique.
List some features that you could use to create names for your fictional
organisms.

_____

_____

_____

_____

_____

_____

_____

_____

Exploration Lab continued

EVALUATE THE PLAN

3 Use your **list of Greek and Latin prefixes, suffixes, and root words** to create two-part scientific names for each organism. Write the names on a separate **piece of paper.** Be sure to write which name goes with which organism.

4 Were you able to think of a unique name for each organism?

_____

_____

_____

5 On a new piece of paper, make a second copy of your names, but write them in random order and do not list the organisms' numbers. Exchange lists with a partner.

6 Look at your partner's list, and try to figure out which names go with which organism. Have your partner check your answers. Were you right? Were there any names that could apply to more than one organism?

_____

_____

_____

_____

_____

_____

_____

_____

_____

_____

_____

_____

_____

_____

_____

Name _____ Class _____ Date _____

Exploration Lab continued

ANALYZE THE RESULTS

7 **Organizing Data** Name a characteristic that all of your organisms share.

_____

DRAW CONCLUSIONS

8 **Identifying Costs and Benefits** Scientific names have two parts, even though it would be easy to give each species one long name. Can you think of how scientists might use two-part names when studying how different species are related?

_____
_____
_____
_____
_____
_____
_____
_____
_____
_____
_____

Connect TO THE ESSENTIAL QUESTION

9 **Evaluating Results** If you gave species 1 a common name, such as *round-face-no-nose*, would any other scientist know which of the organisms you were referring to? Explain your answer.

_____
_____
_____
_____
_____
_____

QUICK LAB `DIRECTED` *Inquiry*

Observing Bacteria `GENERAL`

👥 Small groups

🕐 15 minutes

LAB RATINGS

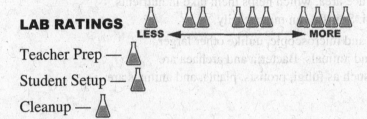

LESS ◄――――――――► MORE

Teacher Prep —

Student Setup —

Cleanup —

MATERIALS

For each group
- compound light microscope
- prepared slides of bacteria with various shapes, such as cocci, bacilli, and spirilla

For each student
- safety goggles

SAFETY INFORMATION

Remind students to review all safety cautions and icons before beginning this lab. Broken microscope slides can cause cuts. Students should immediately report any broken slides.

TEACHER NOTES

In this activity, students will compare, evaluate, and classify bacteria into major groups based on their shapes. While they are waiting for their turn at the microscope, have the students discuss the possible shapes of bacteria that they may see. If possible, avoid large groups so that students are not waiting more than a few minutes. Depending upon the number of students, this activity may take longer than 15 minutes. Consider alternative approaches if time is a concern or microscopes are not available. For example, have bacterial preparations projected on a screen for students to view and compare their observations together. Also, overhead images of bacteria may be available. You may wish to review with students how to correctly use a microscope before they carry out this activity.

Tip This activity may help students better understand that bacteria show a great deal of variation.

Skills Focus Practicing Lab Techniques, Making Observations

MODIFICATION FOR `INDEPENDENT` *Inquiry*

Have students identify questions they have about bacteria. Encourage them to focus on the physical differences between bacteria. Students should perform independent investigations to answer their questions. They should present their findings to the class using a creative method.

My Notes

_____

_____

_____

_____

_____

Quick Lab continued

Answer Key

2. Student drawings should clearly show the shapes of the different bacteria.

3. Sample answer: The round bacteria are cocci. The cylindrical bacteria are bacilli. The spiral-shaped bacteria are spirilla.

4. Sample answer: Bacilli have a large surface area, which helps them take in nutrients. Cocci do not dry out as quickly as bacilli. Spirilla can move easily.

5. Sample answer: Bacteria are unicellular and microscopic, unlike other larger, multicellular organisms such as plants and animals. Bacteria and archaea are prokaryotic, but other living organisms such as fungi, protists, plants, and animals are eukaryotic.

Name _____ Class _____ Date _____

Observing Bacteria

In this lab, you will use a microscope to study the shapes of different kinds of bacteria.

PROCEDURE

1 Using a microscope, observe prepared slides of bacteria.

2 Draw each type of bacteria you see.

OBJECTIVE

• Identify different bacterial shapes.

MATERIALS

For each group

• compound light microscope

• prepared slides of bacteria with various shapes, such as cocci, bacilli, and spirilla

For each student

• safety goggles

3 What different shapes do you see? What are these shapes called?

_____

_____

_____

_____

_____

Quick Lab continued

4 Describe one advantage of each shape of bacteria.

_____
_____
_____
_____
_____

5 Compare the size and structure of bacteria to those of other organisms.

_____
_____
_____
_____
_____
_____
_____
_____

QUICK LAB DIRECTED Inquiry

QUICK LAB DIRECTED Inquiry

Modeling Viral Replication GENERAL

👥 Large groups
🕐 15 minutes

LAB RATINGS

LESS ◄─────────► MORE

Teacher Prep —

Student Setup —

Cleanup —

MATERIALS

- no materials required

My Notes

_____

_____

_____

_____

TEACHER NOTES

In this activity, students will learn how viruses replicate by acting out viral replication as a class.

MODIFICATION FOR GUIDED Inquiry

Help students determine how bacterial reproduction compares to viral replication. Have students form a small circle to represent the DNA within a larger circle of students that represents a cell. Students in the DNA circle should divide to form two small circles within the larger circle. The larger circle then divides into two circles, each one surrounding one smaller circle of "DNA," forming two new cells with the same DNA. Have students discuss how this model differs from the viral replication model.

Skills Focus Making Models, Applying Concepts

MODIFICATION FOR INDEPENDENT Inquiry

Have groups of students come up with a question they have about viral replication. Then, have group members work together to research answers to their question. Have each group share their findings with the class through an oral presentation or poster.

Answer Key

6. Sample answer: The virus has infected the cell by injecting the cell with its genetic material. The cell produces more viruses. Eventually the cell bursts open, releasing the viruses. This is called the lytic cycle.

   Teacher Prompt Do bacteria need host cells to replicate? [No, bacteria reproduce by binary fission. The bacterial DNA replicates in the cytoplasm, and the cell separates into two new cells.]

Modeling Viral Replication

In this lab, you will explore how viruses replicate in cells by acting out the viral replication process with your classmates.

OBJECTIVE

• Describe viral replication.

MATERIALS

• no materials required

PROCEDURE

1 With your classmates, join hands in a circle to form the bacterial cell. One student should remain outside the circle. The student outside the circle represents the virus.

2 The virus enters the cell.

3 The virus picks one person from the cell to move inside the cell and become a virus. The circle closes.

4 Each of the two viruses picks a person to infect. The infected people move inside the cell to become viruses as well. The circle closes.

5 Continue this process until the cell bursts open with viruses.

6 What has happened to the cell? Describe your observations below.

_____

_____

_____

_____

_____

_____

_____

_____

_____

_____

FIELD LAB `DIRECTED Inquiry` AND `GUIDED Inquiry`

Culturing Bacteria from the Environment GENERAL

👥 Individual student

🕐 Two 45-minute class periods

LAB RATINGS

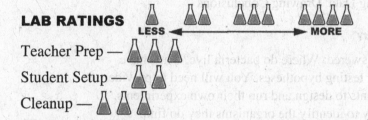

Teacher Prep —

Student Setup —

Cleanup —

SAFETY INFORMATION

Remind students to review all safety cautions and icons before beginning this lab. Remind students to avoid contamination of their samples and of their workspaces and bodies. Students should not open the petri dishes once they have been sealed. Make sure students wear gloves, and wash their hands with soap and water after each lab session.

Although most of the bacteria cultured in a lab such as this do not present a general risk to health or safety, it is important to teach students the proper methods for working with microorganisms and for disposing of materials. Do not dispose of any of this lab's materials in the general classroom waste bins. Prepare specific bins for the disposal of used swabs, gloves, petri dishes, and other contaminated items. Follow your school and/or district guidelines for disposal of potentially hazardous wastes. Wash down all lab surfaces with a diluted bleach solution at the end of each lab session.

TEACHER NOTES

In this activity, students will make predictions about single-celled organisms found in their local environment and then culture them. Pre-poured agar plates can be purchased from a biological supply house. To minimize the risk of contamination from airborne bacteria, have students lift the petri dish lids only slightly when inoculating the agar. An alternative to prepared, sterile agar plates is to prepare liquid nutrient agar that is sterilized and poured into petri dishes. Pre-poured agar plates can be stored for more than one day in a refrigerator; they should be stored in inverted position (upside down) to keep condensation from pooling on the agar surface. Potato slices can also be used instead of agar plates. Keep the swabbed potato slices in labeled, airtight plastic bags. The students should be made clear on what is implied by "sterile." If an incubator is available, the inoculated petri dishes can be incubated at 37°C. This will speed up the bacterial growth.

Tip Explain that students will observe fungal colonies on their plates as well as bacterial colonies. Tell them that bacterial colonies tend to have shiny surfaces, while many fungal colonies look fuzzy.

MATERIALS

For each student
- gloves, protective
- lab apron
- magnifying lens
- marker, permanent
- petri dish containing sterile nutrient agar
- safety goggles
- swab, cotton
- tape, transparent or masking

My Notes

_____

_____

_____

_____

_____

Field Lab continued

Tell the students they will perform an experiment on their own and leave one or more sterile petri dishes uncovered during the activity. They will then cover the dish and store it at the end of the activity. Ask the students during the post-activity discussion to draw conclusions about how colonies formed on the plates that were not purposely inoculated.

Student Tip Treat all bacteria as if they are pathogens. Follow all of your teacher's safety procedures. Never reopen a petri dish that has been inoculated with bacteria. Always wear protective gloves. Do you touch your face, skin, pencils, or other supplies.

Skills Focus Making Observations, Analyzing Data, Drawing Conclusions

MODIFICATION FOR INDEPENDENT Inquiry

Have students formulate the question to be answered: Where do bacteria live? Then have them develop hypotheses and make a plan for testing hypotheses. You will need to provide guidance on sterile technique, but allow students to design and run their own experiments. Have them research the types of bacteria to try to identify the organisms they do find.

Answer Key for DIRECTED Inquiry

FORM A HYPOTHESIS

2. Sample answer: Bacteria will be found on the doorknob because a lot of people touch it every day.

TEST THE HYPOTHESIS

4. The agar should be sterile so that bacteria will be absent when the experiment begins. If the agar was contaminated, we would not know whether the bacteria came from the agar or from the location we swiped.

9. Sample answer: Some variables that may affect bacterial growth include the agar being exposed to air, if the location is used by many people, the moistness of the location, the number of bacteria that stick to the agar, and the temperature at which the agar is kept.

MAKE OBSERVATIONS

10. Answers will vary.

ANALYZE THE RESULTS

11. Answers will vary.

12. Sample answer: Some colonies are big, small, or pinpoint in size. Some colonies are black, white, yellow, or gray in color. Some colonies have a shiny or smooth surface, with edges that are ruffled or smooth.

13. Accept all reasonable answers.

DRAW CONCLUSIONS

14. Accept all reasonable answers.

15. Answers will vary.

16. Accept all reasonable answers.

Field Lab continued

17. Sample answer: Sterilizing surfaces can kill the bacteria on them. Killing the bacteria can help prevent people from coming into contact with them.

Connect TO THE ESSENTIAL QUESTION

18. Sample answer: All bacteria reproduce asexually. This type of reproduction is very fast, which explains why colonies with large numbers of bacteria developed quickly.

Answer Key for GUIDED Inquiry

FORM A HYPOTHESIS

2. Sample answer: Bacteria will be found on the doorknob because a lot of people touch it every day.

TEST THE HYPOTHESIS

4. The agar should be sterile so that bacteria will be absent when the experiment begins. If the agar was contaminated, we would not know whether the bacteria came from the agar or from the location we swiped.

9. Sample answer: Some variables that may affect bacterial growth include the agar being exposed to air, if the location is used by many people, the moistness of the location, the number of bacteria that stick to the agar, and the temperature at which the agar is kept.

MAKE OBSERVATIONS

10. Answers will vary.

ANALYZE THE RESULTS

11. Answers will vary.

12. Sample answer: Some colonies are big, small, or pinpoint in size. Some colonies are black, white, yellow, or gray in color. Some colonies have a shiny or smooth surface, with edges that are ruffled or smooth.

13. Accept all reasonable answers.

DRAW CONCLUSIONS

14. Accept all reasonable answers.

15. Answers will vary.

16. Accept all reasonable answers.

17. Sample answer: Sterilizing surfaces can kill the bacteria on them. Killing the bacteria can help prevent people from coming into contact with them.

Connect TO THE ESSENTIAL QUESTION

18. Sample answer: All bacteria reproduce asexually. This type of reproduction is very fast, which explains why colonies with large numbers of bacteria developed quickly.

Name _____ Class _____ Date _____

Culturing Bacteria from the Environment

In this activity, you will observe some of the bacteria that share your world.
Bacteria are in the soil, in the air, on surfaces, and even on the inside and outside of
your body. When grown in the laboratory, microscopic bacteria form
colonies that you can see.

PROCEDURE

ASK A QUESTION

❶ In this lab, you will investigate the following question: Where
do bacteria live?

FORM A HYPOTHESIS

❷ Choose a certain place in the classroom or bring an object from
home that you think may contain bacteria. Write a hypothesis
that addresses the question above and is specific for the
location/object you chose. State why you think the object may or
may not contain bacteria. Your hypothesis statement should be
in the form, Bacteria will be found to live _____ because
_____.

_____

_____

TEST THE HYPOTHESIS

❸ Obtain one petri dish containing nutrient agar from your teacher.

❹ Why is it important that the nutrient agar be sterile?

_____

_____

_____

_____

❺ Rub one end of a cotton swab on the object or location that you chose to
examine. Then, lift the lid of the petri dish slightly. Lightly rub that same
end of the cotton swab in a zigzag pattern across the agar in the dish.

OBJECTIVES

- Prepare cultures of
  bacteria using agar
  plates.
- Identify places
  where bacteria live.
- Distinguish
  bacterial colonies
  from other
  microorganisms.

MATERIALS

For each student
- gloves, protective
- lab apron
- magnifying lens
- marker, permanent
- petri dish
  containing sterile
  nutrient agar
- safety goggles
- sterile swab, cotton
- tape, transparent or
  masking

Field Lab continued

6 Put the lid back on the petri dish. Secure the petri dish lid with tape. Place the swab and your gloves in the waste disposal container designated by your teacher. Wash your hands.

7 Use a marker to label the bottom of the petri dish to identify the location you chose to swab. Include your initials.

8 Keep the dish upside down in a warm, dark place for about one week. **Caution:** Do not open the petri dish after it is sealed.

9 What factors may affect whether bacteria grow in your petri dish?

_____

_____

_____

_____

_____

MAKE OBSERVATIONS

10 Study your petri dish using a magnifying lens. Compare your petri dish to your classmates' dishes. In the space below, record your observations of your bacterial colonies. Also draw a sketch of your petri dish on a separate sheet of paper.

PETRI DISH OBSERVATIONS

location swabbed	
number of colonies on petri dish	
color of colonies	
size of colonies	
shape of colonies	
appearance of colonies under a magnifying lens	

ANALYZE THE RESULTS

11 **Comparing Samples** How does the bacterial growth in your dish compare with your classmates' dishes?

_____

_____

_____

_____

_____

Field Lab continued

⑫ Describing Data What do the bacterial colonies look like?

_____

_____

_____

⑬ Examining Predictions Which locations caused the most bacterial growth? The least bacterial growth? Why do you think this was the case for each?

_____

_____

_____

_____

_____

DRAW CONCLUSIONS

⑭ Defending Hypotheses Was your hypothesis supported by your observations? Explain.

_____

_____

_____

_____

_____

_____

⑮ Classifying Organisms Use the table on the next page to find out what kinds of bacteria might have made the colonies in your petri dish. Record the name that best fits your results. Explain why you might not have been able to match all of your colonies to one described in the table.

_____

_____

_____

_____

Field Lab continued

KEY FOR THE IDENTIFICATION OF SOME COMMON BACTERIA

Bacterial genus	Colony appearance (on agar plates)				
	Average size (mm)	Shape	Elevation	Color	Surface
Bacillus	2	circular	flat	cream	smooth
Escherichia	2	circular	convex	cream	smooth, may look a little "bumpy"
Serratia	1	circular	convex	red/orange	shiny/wet looking
Streptococcus	1	circular	convex	white or yellow	smooth
Proteus	2	circular	flat	cream	smooth, may look like colonies "spread" across plate (called swarming)
Staphylococcus	0.5	circular	convex	white	smooth and shiny

16 Evaluating Methods If you were going to perform another investigation, what would you change to obtain better results? Explain.

_____

_____

_____

17 Applying Observations Use your results to explain how sterilizing surfaces can reduce the spread of bacterial illness.

_____

_____

_____

_____

Connect TO THE ESSENTIAL QUESTION

18 Making Inferences What method of reproduction do all bacteria use? How do the colonies you observed support what you learned about reproduction in bacteria?

_____

_____

_____

_____

_____

FIELD LAB GUIDED *Inquiry*

Culturing Bacteria from the Environment

In this activity, you will observe some of the bacteria that share your world. Bacteria are in the soil, in the air, and on the surfaces of leaves, rocks, and puddles. After collecting an item from the environment, you will use it to grow bacteria on an agar plate. When grown in the laboratory, microscopic bacteria form colonies that you can see and possibly identify.

PROCEDURE

ASK A QUESTION

❶ In this lab, you will investigate the following question: Where do bacteria live in outside environments?

FORM A HYPOTHESIS

❷ Choose a certain place outside—around either your school or your home—that you think may contain bacteria. Write a hypothesis that addresses the question above and is specific for the location you chose. Your hypothesis statement should include the word "because."

_____

_____

TEST THE HYPOTHESIS

❸ Obtain one petri dish containing nutrient agar from your teacher.

❹ Why is it important that the nutrient agar be sterile?

_____

_____

_____

❺ Rub one end of a cotton swab on the object or location that you chose to examine. Then, lift the lid of the petri dish slightly. Lightly rub that same end of the cotton swab in a zigzag pattern across the agar in the dish.

❻ Put the lid back on the petri dish. Secure the petri dish lid with tape. Place the swab and your gloves in the waste disposal container designated by your teacher. Wash your hands.

OBJECTIVES

- Prepare cultures of bacteria using agar plates.
- Identify places where bacteria live.
- Distinguish bacterial colonies from other microorganisms.

MATERIALS

For each student
- gloves, protective
- lab apron
- magnifying lens
- marker, permanent
- petri dish containing sterile nutrient agar
- safety goggles
- swab, cotton
- tape, transparent or masking

Field Lab continued

7 Use a marker to label the bottom of the petri dish to identify the location you chose to swab. Include your initials.

8 Keep the dish upside down in a warm, dark place for about one week. **Caution:** Do not open the petri dish after it is sealed.

9 What factors may affect whether bacteria grow in your petri dish?

_____

_____

_____

MAKE OBSERVATIONS

10 Study your petri dish using a magnifying lens. In the space below, record your observations of your bacterial colonies.

_____

_____

ANALYZE THE RESULTS

11 **Comparing Samples** How does the bacterial growth in your dish compare with bacterial growth in your classmates' dishes?

_____

_____

12 **Recognizing Patterns** What are some characteristics that can be used to differentiate between bacterial colonies?

_____

_____

13 **Examining Hypotheses** Which locations resulted in the most bacterial growth? The least bacterial growth? Why do you think this trend occurred?

_____

_____

DRAW CONCLUSIONS

14 **Defending Hypotheses** Was your hypothesis supported by your observations? Explain your answer.

_____

_____

_____

Field Lab continued

15 **Classifying Organisms** Use the table below to find out what kinds of bacteria might have made the colonies in your petri dish. Record the name that best fits your results. Explain why you might not have been able to match all of your colonies to one described in the table.

_____

_____

KEY FOR THE IDENTIFICATION OF SOME COMMON BACTERIA

Bacterial genus	Colony appearance (on agar plates)				
	Average size (mm)	Shape	Elevation	Color	Surface
Bacillus	2	circular	flat	cream	smooth
Escherichia	2	circular	convex	cream	smooth, may look a little "bumpy"
Serratia	1	circular	convex	red/orange	shiny/wet looking
Streptococcus	1	circular	convex	white or yellow	smooth
Proteus	2	circular	flat	cream	smooth, may look like colonies "spread" across plate (called swarming)
Staphylococcus	0.5	circular	convex	white	smooth and shiny

16 **Evaluating Methods** If you were going to perform another investigation, what would you change to obtain better results? Explain.

_____

_____

17 **Applying Observations** Use your results to explain how sterilizing surfaces can reduce the spread of bacterial illness.

_____

_____

Connect **TO THE ESSENTIAL QUESTION**

18 **Making Inferences** What method of reproduction do all bacteria use? How do the colonies you observed support what you learned about reproduction in bacteria?

_____

_____

_____

_____

What Do Protists Look Like? GENERAL

👤 Individual student
⏱ 30 minutes

LAB RATINGS

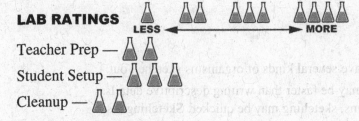

LESS ←————————→ MORE

Teacher Prep — 🝧🝧

Student Setup — 🝧🝧🝧

Cleanup — 🝧🝧

SAFETY INFORMATION

Remind students to review all safety cautions and icons before beginning this activity. Tell students not to drink the pond water or taste the ProtoSlo® solution. Care should be taken handling microscope slides and coverslips. Check for known mold or fungi allergies among students before conducting this lab. Have an eyewash available, and instruct students to wipe up all spills immediately.

TEACHER NOTES

In this activity, students will research a type of protist, such as a paramecium, amoeba, or volvox. Then they will compare their protists based on structural features.

A day before this activity, collect samples of water from sources such as a pool formed from melting ice or snow, a pond, mud from a garden, or a neglected vase of flowers. You could also have students collect samples several days beforehand. You may want to have students work in small groups if there are not enough microscopes for the entire class. Microscope slides may be disposed of in the garbage or carefully disassembled, washed, and reused.

Tip This activity may help students better understand how organisms are classified according to similar characteristics.

Skills Focus Practicing Lab Techniques, Making Observations, Drawing Conclusions

MODIFICATION FOR GUIDED *Inquiry*

Instead of giving students the instructions for how to observe and describe the protists, have them develop their own procedure for making observations and collecting data. Have them develop a classification system for the protists they observe. Students should provide a procedure for collecting and organizing data, and with teacher approval they should carry out their procedures. They should also answer Questions 8–11.

MATERIALS

For each student
• gloves
• lab apron
• microscope slide (concave or well)
• plastic coverslip
• plastic dropper
• pond water
• protist-slowing agent
• safety goggles

My Notes

_____

_____

_____

_____

_____

Quick Lab continued

MODIFICATION FOR INDEPENDENT Inquiry

Have students think about how they can observe and classify microscopic organisms. They should develop their own procedure for collecting samples, making observations, recording data, and classifying organisms. With teacher approval, they should carry out their procedures and present their conclusions in a lab report.

Answer Key

5. Answers will vary.

6. Answers will vary, but students should have several kinds of organisms sketched out.

7. Sample answer: Sketching observations may be faster than writing descriptive details. When you are observing moving organisms, sketching may be quicker. Sketching also adds to a written description.

8. Answers may vary.

9. Sample answer: Yes, the organisms are alive. The organisms are moving, which suggests that they are alive.

10. Answers may vary, but most of these microscopic organisms, if not all, are single-celled organisms.

11. Sample answer: Many of the organisms were green, and some were moving with flagella. The organisms were different in shape and size.
    Teacher Prompt How might you classify these organisms into groups? Sample answer: by their method of movement; by color, size, and shape; or by the number of cells they contain

Name _____ Class _____ Date _____

What Do Protists Look Like?

In this activity, you will identify, compare, and classify common protists found in pond water. You will construct a microscope slide of pond water samples and then use a microscope to observe the sample.

PROCEDURE

① Use a **plastic eyedropper** to place *one drop* of **pond water** onto a **microscope slide.** To collect a sample of pond water, squeeze the bulb of the eyedropper before putting it into the pond water. Insert the tip of the dropper in the water, and then release the bulb slightly to collect a sample.

② Add a drop of **protist slowing agent** to the slide.

③ Place a **plastic coverslip** on the slide. To prevent bubbles, place one edge of the coverslip on the slide and then slowly lower the coverslip over the water sample.

④ Place the slide under a **microscope**, and observe the sample on low power.

⑤ Find an organism in the liquid on the slide. Observe the organism under high power to get a closer look. Sketch the organism as you see it under high power.

OBJECTIVES
- Identify common protists.
- Describe the features of common protists.
- Compare common protists.
- Classify common protists.

MATERIALS
For each student
- gloves
- lab apron
- microscope slide (concave or well)
- plastic coverslip
- plastic dropper
- pond water
- protist slowing agent
- safety goggles

Name _____ Class _____ Date _____

Quick Lab continued

6 Set the microscope back to low power, and find other organisms in the liquid. When you find an organism, return the microscope to high power and sketch each new organism you find. Repeat this procedure several times.

7 What is the benefit of sketching your observations?

_____

_____

_____

_____

_____

8 How many different kinds of organisms do you see?

_____

_____

_____

Quick Lab continued

9 Are the organisms alive? Support your answer with evidence.

_____

_____

_____

_____

_____

_____

10 How many cells does each organism appear to have?

_____

_____

_____

11 What characteristics do these organisms have in common? How do they differ?

_____

_____

_____

_____

_____

_____

_____

_____

_____

QUICK LAB GUIDED *Inquiry*

Observing a Mushroom's Spores and Hyphae GENERAL

👥 Student pairs

🕐 30 minutes

LAB RATINGS

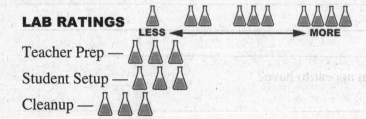

LESS ◄─────────► MORE

Teacher Prep —

Student Setup —

Cleanup —

MATERIALS

For each pair
- incubator/(optional)
- microscope or magnifying lens
- mushroom
- paper, white (2 sheets)
- petri dish with fruit-juice agar
- ruler, metric
- tape, masking
- tape, transparent
- tweezers

For each student
- safety goggles

SAFETY INFORMATION

Remind students to review all safety cautions and icons before beginning this lab. Before beginning this lab, check for any mushroom allergies among students. Do not use muschrooms gathered from the wild. Suitable mushrooms can be found in the produce section of a grocery store.

TEACHER NOTES

In this activity, students will work in pairs to examine the structure of a mushroom. Pre-poured agar plates can be purchased from a biological supply house. To minimize the risk of contamination from airborne bacteria, have students lift the petri dish lids only slightly when treating the agar. If you do not have an incubator, place the petri dishes in a warm place, out of drafts and shielded from direct sunlight.

After 24 hours of incubation students may see a mass of hyphae, a mycelium, on the agar in the petri dish. Depending on incubation conditions, it may take a little longer than this for observable hyphae to form.

Tip This activity may help students understand the structure of fungi, in general, and the structure of a basidiomycete, in particular. The mushrooms they will be examining are the aboveground fruiting bodies (structures that form spores for reproduction) of one species of fungus. The main body of the fungus grows in the soil as a mass of hyphae. The mass of hyphae in the belowground portion of the fungus is called a mycelium.

Student Tip A mushroom is a fruiting body formed by a particular species of fungus. The main body of the fungus grows in the soil. When it is time for the fungus to reproduce, the fungus produces mushrooms that grow aboveground. Like the flower of a plant, a mushroom produces the reproductive structures of the fungus. Flowers produce seeds, and mushrooms produce spores.

Skills Focus Making Observations, Interpreting Observations

My Notes

_____

_____

_____

_____

_____

Quick Lab continued

MODIFICATION FOR INDEPENDENT *Inquiry*

Have students research other kinds of fruiting bodies produced by fungi. Examples include puff balls, morels, and the ear-like structure of the shelf fungi. They can make drawings in which they label the spore-producing fruiting body and the mycelium that is either growing underground or in decomposing tissue such as that of a dead tree. This will reinforce the concept that a mushroom is only part of the whole body of a fungus and that different fungi produce different types of fruiting bodies and reproductive structures.

Answer Key

4. Accept all reasonable answers.

6. Sample answer: The gill was covered with tiny structures that stick up and have spores on them. The hyphae look like hairs or strings.
Teacher Prompt What appears to be covering the surfaces of the gill?

7. Sample answer: Hyphae, which first develop from germinating spores, grow together to form the main body of the mushroom. The hyphae from a piece of a mushroom can continue to grow and form a new mycelium.
Teacher Prompt Where do you think this part of a fungus, which will later make mushrooms, would grow?

8. Sample answer: The print on the white paper is a spore print produced by basidiospores being released from the structures that cover the gills.

QUICK LAB GUIDED Inquiry

Observing a Mushroom's Spores and Hyphae

In this lab, you will observe some of the unique structures of a mushroom produced by a member of the kingdom Fungi. Fungi share many characteristics with plants. For example, most fungi live on land and cannot move from place to place. But fungi have several unique features that suggest that they are not closely related to any other kingdom of organisms.

PROCEDURE

1 Obtain a mushroom from your teacher. Carefully pull the cap of the mushroom from the stem.

2 Using tweezers, remove one of the gills from the underside of the cap. Place the gill on a sheet of white paper.

3 Place the mushroom cap gill-side down on the other sheet of paper. Use masking tape to keep the mushroom cap in place. Set the paper aside for at least 24 hours.

4 Use tweezers to take several 1 centimeter (cm) pieces from the stem, and place these pieces in your petri dish. Cover the petri dish. Draw the appearance of the plate below. Incubate the dish overnight.

OBJECTIVES

- Examine the parts of a mushroom.
- Describe observations of the structures of a mushroom.

MATERIALS

For each pair
- incubator/(optional)
- microscope or magnifying lens
- mushroom
- paper, white (2 sheets)
- petri dish with fruit-juice agar
- ruler, metric
- tape, masking
- tape, transparent
- tweezers

For each student
- safety goggles

5 Use tweezers to gently pull the remaining mushroom stem apart lengthwise. The individual fibers or strings that you see are the hyphae, which form the structure of the fungus. Place a thin strand next to the gill that you removed from the cap.

6 Use a magnifying lens or microscope to observe the gill and the hyphae from the stem. Describe the structures that you saw on the gill and hyphae.

_____

_____

Quick Lab continued

❼ After at least 24 hours, observe the petri dish and compare it with your original drawing of the petri dish. Record any changes that happened in the petri dish by making a new drawing to show the changes. Explain how these changes are related to the way fungi grow.

_____

_____

_____

_____

❽ After at least 24 hours, carefully remove the mushroom cap from the paper. Place pieces of transparent tape over the print left behind on the paper. Record your observations. What makes up the print that was left on the white paper?

_____

_____

_____

_____

EXPLORATION LAB GUIDED Inquiry **AND** INDEPENDENT Inquiry

Survey of Reproduction in Protists and Fungi ADVANCED

👥 Student pairs

🕐 45 minutes

LAB RATINGS

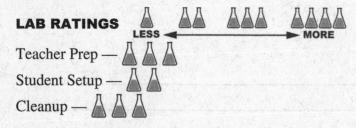

LESS ← → MORE

Teacher Prep —

Student Setup —

Cleanup —

SAFETY INFORMATION

Remind students to review all safety cautions and icons before beginning this lab. Instruct students to clean up any water spills immediately because slippery floors can be dangerous. Inform students that they should wear safety goggles, a lab apron, and hand protection if they prepare their own yeast suspensions.

TEACHER NOTES

In this activity, students will examine prepared slides of protists and fungi under a microscope to observe the physical structures and reproductive characteristics of these organisms. Prepared slides can be ordered from most online biological supply vendors.

For the protist slides, it is ideal to obtain some slides showing asexual reproduction, such as binary fission or fragmentation, and some showing sexual reproduction, such as conjugation. For example, a prepared slide of a *Paramecium* undergoing binary fission and a prepared slide of a *Paramecium* undergoing conjugation would be appropriate. Before class, label the binary fission and conjugation slides: *Paramecium Slide A* and *Paramecium Slide B*, respectively. For the independent inquiry option, students will research and decide on the protist organisms to be ordered.

For the fungi slides, it is ideal to obtain a slide showing sexual reproduction. Under the right conditions, bread molds will undergo sexual reproduction. You can order prepared bread mold slides from most biological supply vendors; any variety of the *Rhizopus* fungus would be appropriate. Be sure that the slide shows sexual reproduction (wherein the *Rhizopus* form *Zygosporangia*). For the independent inquiry option, students will research and decide on the fungus organisms to be ordered. Clarify with students, however, that some organisms cannot be studied.

MATERIALS

For each group
- cover slip
- eyedropper
- microscope, compound
- microscope slide
- microscope slide, prepared, *Paramecium* binary fission
- microscope slide, prepared, *Paramecium* conjugation
- microscope slide, prepared, *Rhizopus* sexual reproduction
- yeast, active dry

For each student
- lab apron
- safety goggles

My Notes

_____

_____

_____

_____

_____

Exploration Lab continued

In addition to observing prepared slides, students will prepare their own wet mount of a yeast suspension to observe live yeast budding under a microscope. You may wish to prepare the yeast suspension for students ahead of class. To do this, dissolve one packet of active dry yeast into 300 millileters (mL) of warm water in a beaker. Add 1 teaspoon (tsp) of granulated sugar to the solution and stir the solution vigorously. Then, allow the solution to incubate at room temperature for 30 minutes (min), stirring occasionally. For the independent inquiry option, allow students to prepare their own yeast suspension. The yeast suspension is not dangerous to the students and can be discarded down the drain.

Tip Be sure that students stir the yeast suspension before obtaining a sample for their wet mounts. As the suspension sits, the yeast will tend to settle at the bottom of the beaker. Demonstrate a proper technique for preparing a wet mount.

Skills Focus Practicing Lab Techniques, Making Observations, Analyzing Samples

MODIFICATION FOR DIRECTED Inquiry

Order the prepared *Paramecium* and *Rhizopus* slides in advance and prepare the yeast suspension 30 min prior to the start of class. Have pairs of students examine the prepared slides under a microscope and make sketches of each slide. For the protist slides, students should identify the type of reproduction taking place (sexual or asexual), and they should provide evidence for their reasoning. For the fungi slides, students should be sure to identify and label as many structures as they can, such as hyphae and spores, and they should identify the type of reproduction taking place (sexual or asexual). Then, have students prepare a wet mount of the yeast suspension. To do this, students should apply two drops of yeast suspension to a clean glass slide and then cover the slide. Students should observe and sketch the slide under a microscope, and they should identify the type of reproduction taking place on the slide (budding). Finally, have students compare and contrast the different types of reproduction that they observed for each slide.

Answer Key for GUIDED Inquiry

DEVELOP A PLAN

2. Accept all reasonable answers.
Teacher Prompt How would adjusting the level of magnification on your microscope help you make observations?

MAKE OBSERVATIONS

3. Accept all reasonable answers.
Teacher Prompt How would drawing detailed sketches help you analyze the structures of the organisms?

DEVELOP A PLAN

4. Accept all reasonable answers.
Teacher Prompt What do you think will happen if you put too much of the concentrated yeast solution on a slide?

Exploration Lab continued

MAKE OBSERVATIONS

5. Accept all reasonable answers.

ANALYZE RESULTS

6. Students should be able to identify and label hyphae, spores, nuclei, cilia, flagella, organelles, and cell walls.

7. Sample answer: Slide A shows the *Paramecia* joined at the cell wall near the narrow ends of their cells, while Slide B showed two *Paramecia* joined at the long side of the cell wall.

8. Sample answer: The *Rhizopus* slide shows two hyphae fusing together to form one dark structure. The yeast slide shows yeast cells joined at the cell walls, and they appear to be splitting into two.

DRAW CONCLUSIONS

9. Sample answer: Slide A shows binary fission (asexual reproduction), and Slide B shows sexual reproduction. I think this because the two cells in Slide A are joined at the narrow end and both seem to have a nuclei, so this is probably binary fission. Slide B shows the *Paramecia* joined at the long side of the cells, so this is most likely sexual reproduction. The *Rhizopus* shows sexual reproduction because it shows the two hyphae fusing together. The yeast slide shows budding (asexual reproduction) because parts of the cells are pinching off to form new cells.

10. Sample answer: I could stain the yeast suspension on the wet mount in order to see individual cells more clearly.
    Teacher Prompt What type of substance do scientists sometimes use to help make cells easier to observe on a slide?

Connect TO THE ESSENTIAL QUESTION

11. Accept all reasonable answers.

Answer Key for INDEPENDENT Inquiry

DEVELOP A PLAN

2. Accept all reasonable answers.
   Teacher Prompt One type of protist is a *Paramecium*, and one type of fungus is bread mold, which is also known as *Rhizopus*. What kinds of reproduction do these organisms undergo?

3. Accept all reasonable answers.

MAKE OBSERVATIONS

4. Accept all reasonable answers.
   Teacher Prompt How would drawing detailed sketches help you analyze the structures of the organisms?

Exploration Lab continued

DEVELOP A PLAN

5. Accept all reasonable answers.
Teacher Prompt What do you think will happen if you put too much of the concentrated yeast solution on a slide?

MAKE OBSERVATIONS

6. Accept all reasonable answers.

ANALYZE RESULTS

7. Students should be able to identify and label hyphae, spores, nuclei, cilia, flagella, organelles, and cell walls.

8. Accept all reasonable answers.

9. Accept all reasonable answers.

DRAW CONCLUSIONS

10. Sample answer: Slide A shows binary fission (asexual reproduction), and Slide B shows sexual reproduction. I think this because the two cells in Slide A are joined at the narrow end and both seem to have a nuclei, so this is probably binary fission. Slide B shows the *Paramecia* joined at the long side of the cells, so this is most likely sexual reproduction. The *Rhizopus* shows sexual reproduction because it shows the two hyphae fusing together. The yeast slide shows budding (asexual reproduction) because parts of the cells are pinching off to form new cells.

11. Accept all reasonable answers.
Teacher Prompt Are there any characteristics of a particular slide that are very different from the other slides? Are some slides similar? How could you use these characteristics to determine the type of reproduction taking place in an unlabeled slide?

Connect TO THE ESSENTIAL QUESTION

12. Accept all reasonable answers.

Name _____ Class _____ Date _____

Survey of Reproduction in Protists and Fungi

In this lab, you will examine different protists and fungi under a microscope to observe the reproductive characteristics of these organisms. The protists you will examine are members of the genus *Paramecium*, and the fungus you will examine is a type of bread mold from the genus *Rhizopus*. You will also prepare a wet mount of live yeast cells, another type of fungus, to observe how they reproduce.

PROCEDURE

ASK A QUESTION

❶ Protists and fungi reproduce sexually and asexually. What are the characteristics of sexual and asexual reproduction in these organisms?

DEVELOP A PLAN

❷ You will examine prepared slides of reproducing *Paramecium* and *Rhizopus* organisms. Describe how you will observe and record your observations of these slides.

_____

_____

_____

_____

OBJECTIVES

- Observe and describe how protists reproduce.
- Observe and describe how fungi reproduce.
- Identify different types of fungi and describe their structures.

MATERIALS

For each group
- cover slip
- eyedropper
- microscope, compound
- microscope slide
- microscope slide, prepared, *Paramecium* Slide A
- microscope slide, prepared, *Paramecium* Slide B
- microscope slide, prepared, *Rhizopus*
- yeast suspension

For each student
- lab apron
- safety goggles

Exploration Lab continued

MAKE OBSERVATIONS

3 With teacher approval, carry out your procedures for examining the prepared slides. Record all of your observations in the space provided.

DEVELOP A PLAN

4 Most bakers use a type of active yeast for bread-making. This yeast is a fungus. Your instructor has prepared a yeast suspension that contains reproducing yeast organisms. Describe the steps you will take to prepare a wet mount of the yeast suspension, and explain how you will observe and record your observations of the slide.

_____

_____

_____

_____

MAKE OBSERVATIONS

5 With teacher approval, carry out your procedures for preparing and examining the wet mount. Record all of your observations in the space provided.

ANALYZE RESULTS

6 **Analyzing Observations** Examine your sketches of the protist and fungi slides. Label all of the cell structures you can identify.

Exploration Lab continued

⑦ Describing Samples Describe the characteristics of the two *Paramecium* samples. How are these similar and different?

_____

_____

⑧ Describing Samples Describe the characteristics of the *Rhizopus* and baker's yeast samples. How are these similar and different?

_____

_____

DRAW CONCLUSIONS

⑨ Interpreting Results Determine the types of reproduction taking place in each of the samples you examined. Do you think the reproduction is sexual or asexual? If it is asexual, is it budding, binary fission, or fragmentation? Explain your reasoning.

_____

_____

_____

⑩ Evaluating Methods How could you modify the procedures in this investigation to obtain more detailed observations of the slides?

_____

_____

_____

Connect TO THE ESSENTIAL QUESTION

⑪ Describing Organisms Summarize some features of protists and fungi that distinguish them from other organisms.

_____

_____

_____

_____

EXPLORATION LAB INDEPENDENT *Inquiry*

Survey of Reproduction in Protists and Fungi

In this lab, you will research protists and fungi that reproduce sexually and asexually and use this information to construct a list of protist and fungi to examine under a microscope. You will then conduct your examinations of different protists and fungi to observe their reproductive characteristics. You will also prepare a wet mount of live yeast cells, another type of fungus, to observe how they reproduce.

PROCEDURE

ASK A QUESTION

❶ Protists and fungi reproduce sexually and asexually. What are the characteristics of sexual and asexual reproduction in these organisms?

DEVELOP A PLAN

❷ Your instructor can order prepared microscope slides that show different protists and fungi reproducing in different ways. For this investigation, you will want to observe protists and fungi reproducing both sexually and asexually. Research different types of protists and determine which types reproduce sexually and asexually, and repeat this research for fungi. Then, brainstorm a list of organisms that you would like to observe for this investigation.

_____

_____

_____

_____

❸ Describe a set of procedures that you will follow to observe and record your observations of the slides.

_____

_____

_____

_____

_____

OBJECTIVES

• Observe and describe how protists reproduce.

• Observe and describe how fungi reproduce.

• Identify different types of fungi and describe their structures.

MATERIALS

For each group
• cover slip
• eyedropper
• microscope, compound
• microscope slide
• yeast suspension
For each student
• lab apron
• safety goggles

Exploration Lab continued

MAKE OBSERVATIONS

4 Once the slides have arrived, carry out your procedures for examining the prepared slides. Record all of your observations in the space provided.

DEVELOP A PLAN

5 Most bakers use a type of active yeast for bread-making. This yeast is a fungus. Your instructor has prepared a yeast suspension that contains reproducing yeast organisms. Describe the steps you will take to prepare a wet mount of the yeast suspension, and explain how you will observe and record your observations of the slide.

_____

_____

_____

_____

MAKE OBSERVATIONS

6 With teacher approval, carry out your procedures for preparing and examining the wet mount. Record your observations in the space provided.

Name _____ Class _____ Date _____

Exploration Lab continued

ANALYZE RESULTS

7 **Analyzing Observations** Examine your sketches of the protist and fungi slides. Label all of the cell structures you can identify.

_____

_____

_____

_____

8 **Describing Samples** Describe the characteristics of the protist samples. How are these similar and different?

_____

_____

_____

9 **Describing Samples** Describe the characteristics of the fungus samples. How are these similar and different?

_____

_____

_____

_____

DRAW CONCLUSIONS

10 **Evaluating Results** List the types of reproduction taking place in each of the cells that you examined. Is the reproduction sexual or asexual? If it is asexual, is it budding, binary fission, or fragmentation? Explain.

_____

_____

_____

_____

_____

_____

Exploration Lab continued

⑪ **Developing Conclusions** Based on your observations, what do you think are some characteristics of each type of reproduction that you observed in this investigation?

_____

_____

_____

_____

_____

_____

Connect TO THE ESSENTIAL QUESTION

⑫ **Describing Organisms** Summarize some features of protists and fungi that distinguish them from other organisms.

_____

_____

_____

_____

QUICK LAB GUIDED Inquiry

Investigating Flower Parts GENERAL

👥 Individual student

🕐 30 minutes

LAB RATINGS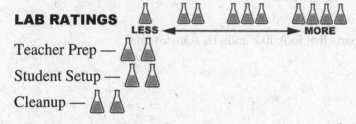

LESS ←——————————→ MORE

Teacher Prep —

Student Setup —

Cleanup —

MATERIALS

For each student
• flowers
• magnifying lens
• scalpel

My Notes

_____

_____

_____

_____

_____

SAFETY INFORMATION

Remind students to review all safety cautions and icons before beginning
this lab. Instruct students to always use care when working with a scalpel
and always cut in a direction away from themselves. If any students have
pollen allergies, have them wear lab gloves and a surgical mask to limit their
contact with pollen. Make sure students wash their hands thoroughly after
handling plants.

TEACHER NOTES

In this activity, students will observe flowers and draw pictures to record what they
observe. Consider contacting local florists and asking for donations of flowers they can
no longer sell.

Tip This activity may help students better understand the parts of a flower. You may wish
to have a diagram of the parts of a flower available for students to refer to if necessary.

Skills Focus Making Observations, Practicing Lab Techniques

MODIFICATION FOR DIRECTED Inquiry

Provide students with two flowers of the same type. Have them attach one flower to a piece
of posterboard and label the visible parts of the flower. Then, guide students as they dissect
the other flower. Have them attach the dissected parts of this flower to the posterboard and
label them. Display finished projects in the class.

MODIFICATION FOR INDEPENDENT Inquiry

Remind students that scientists use all their senses when making observations. Ask students
what other senses they can use to observe the flowers. Have them record their observations.
Encourage them to be as specific as possible when describing the flower. For example, if
they are observing a pink rose, have them describe the variations of color and the texture
and shape of each petal instead of just saying "pink." Have student volunteers share their
observations with the class.

Answer Key

1. Accept all reasonable answers. Be sure that students label the following parts: sepals, petals, stamen, anther, pistil.

2. Accept all reasonable answers.

3. Answers will vary depending on the type of flower used.

4. Answers will vary depending on the type of flower used.

5. Sample answer: I would look for pollen, parts that look like anthers, stamens, and pistils in the center of the structure.

QUICK LAB GUIDED *Inquiry*

Investigate Flower Parts

In this activity, you will dissect a flower to make observations about flower parts.

PROCEDURE

❶ Examine the flower you are given. Try to notice as many details as you can. Draw a diagram of the flower and label its parts.

OBJECTIVES

- Observe the parts of a flower.
- Draw a model of the parts of a flower.

MATERIALS

For each student

- flowers
- magnifying lens
- scalpel

❷ Use the scalpel to carefully dissect your flower. Sort the parts. Use the hand lens to examine each one. Draw and label one example of each part.

Quick Lab continued

③ Choose one flower part. Write a detailed description of that part.

_____

_____

_____

_____

④ Was there a pattern to the arrangement of flower parts? Explain.

_____

_____

_____

⑤ Based on your experience, what would you look for if you were trying to decide whether a structure on an unfamiliar plant was a flower or not?

_____

_____

_____

_____

QUICK LAB GUIDED *Inquiry*

Observing Transport GENERAL

👥 Individual student

🕐 30 minutes plus 5 minutes on the following day

LAB RATINGS

LESS ←→ MORE

Teacher Prep —

Student Setup —

Cleanup —

MATERIALS

For teacher
- knife

For each student
- beaker or jar
- celery stalk with leaves
- food coloring
- lab apron
- pencils, colored
- safety goggles
- water

My Notes
_____
_____
_____
_____
_____

SAFETY INFORMATION

Remind students to review all safety cautions and icons before beginning this lab. To avoid having students handle knives, it is best if you cut the celery stalks for students. Spilled water on the floor creates a slipping hazard, so instruct students to clean spills immediately and have paper towels available for this purpose. Food coloring will stain clothing, so have students wear aprons. Make sure students wash and dry their hands after handling food coloring and celery.

TEACHER NOTES

In this activity, students will observe vascular transport in a celery stalk placed in a glass of colored water. Leafy celery stalks work best in this activity although white flowers such as carnations also work well.

It works best to cut celery (or carnation stem) at the time students will be carrying out their experiments. You may want to have a cutting station set up where students can come to receive their celery stalk from you.

Tip This activity may help students better understand vascular transport. Before beginning this activity, you may wish to review the structures that distinguish certain plants as belonging to the vascular plant group (xylem and phloem).

Skills Focus Making Observations, Interpreting Results

MODIFICATION FOR DIRECTED *Inquiry*

Walk students through the process of placing their celery in the colored water and making observations. Have students draw their observations at each step in the process.

MODIFICATION FOR INDEPENDENT *Inquiry*

Ask students how water moves through a plant. Tell students to design a model to show vascular transport in a plant. Designs should include materials students plan to use and a detailed procedure which includes how they plan to communicate results. Approve all reasonable plans and allow students to carry them out.

Quick Lab continued

Answer Key

1. Sample answer: I will mix 5 drops of food coloring with 100 mL water. Then I will place the celery stalk in colored water and observe as the colored water moves through the stalk.
   Teacher Prompt Look at the bottom of the stalk of celery. Will nutrients be able to get through the bottom? How can you make the clear water more easily observable?

3. Check students' observations. They will be able to see the colored water moving through the celery stalk.

5. Check students' observations. The colored water should have traveled to the leaves.

6. Sample answer: The colored water moved through tubes in the stem to the leaves.

7. Sample answer: The stem provides support for the plant and contains the tissues that transport materials throughout the plant.

QUICK LAB GUIDED *Inquiry*

Observing Transport

Celery is a vascular plant. All vascular plants have tissues that
function to move water and other small molecules through the plant.
In this activity, you will design a model to observe how nutrients move
through a vascular plant's transport tissues.

PROCEDURE

1 How can you show vascular transport using the celery stalk and
the other materials provided? Write a step-by-step procedure.
Include how you will record your observations in your
procedure.

_____

_____

_____

_____

_____

2 Show your plan to your teacher. Once your teacher has approved your plan,
carry it out.

3 Observe your experiment every 5 minutes for 30 minutes. Record your
observations in the manner detailed in your plan.

4 Set your experiment aside overnight.

OBJECTIVES

- Design an experiment.
- Observe transport in a
  plant.

MATERIALS

For each student
- beaker or jar
- celery stalk with
  leaves
- food coloring
- lab apron
- pencils, colored
- safety goggles
- water

Quick Lab continued

5 Observe your experiment after 24 hours. What do you see? Record your observations.

6 How did your experiment show vascular transport?

_____

_____

_____

_____

7 Based on your observations, what is the function of a plant's stem?

_____

_____

_____

_____

QUICK LAB DIRECTED **Inquiry**

Investigating Plant Pigments GENERAL

👥 Student pairs

🕐 45 minutes

LAB RATINGS

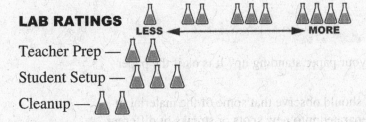

LESS ⟵————————⟶ MORE

Teacher Prep —

Student Setup —

Cleanup —

SAFETY INFORMATION

Remind students to review all safety cautions and icons before beginning this lab. If students use a hair dryer to dry the pigment, be sure that they keep it away from the isopropyl alcohol. Make sure students wash their hands carefully after handling the isopropyl alcohol and plants.

TEACHER NOTES

In this activity, students will crush fresh spinach leaves with a mortar and pestle and make an extract of the cellular contents using isopropyl alcohol. They subject this extract to paper chromatography using isopropyl alcohol as the mobile phase (migrating solvent). Students will observe that the dark green extract they begin with separates into a series of streaks and dots in their chromatograms that have a range of colors.

Because the preparation phase of this activity is fairly time consumptive and you may not have enough mortars and pestles to distribute to every pair, you may wish to prepare the spinach extract for students just before class. A blender can also be used to prepare the extract. You can also have students blow on their pigment extract rather than having them use a hair dryer.

The chromatography works best if the leaf extract is applied in the smallest possible amounts so that the spot produced on the paper has a very small diameter. Typical eyedroppers will produce very large spots, so it is recommended that narrow bore Pasteur pipettes or capillary tubes be used for the spotting. If filter paper is not available, coffee filters may be used.

Tip Show pictures of autumn leaves. Ask students to describe the color and ask what color they think the leaves would have been in spring. (green) Ask them to make an inference about the pigments in a leaf based on this observation. (Plants must contain other pigments besides chlorophyll.)

Student Tip What leaf colors have you seen? What pigment colors do you think were in these leaves?

Skills Focus Making Observations, Practicing Lab Techniques

MATERIALS

For each pair
- beakers, 250 mL (2)
- eyedropper
- filter paper strip, 12 cm × 3 cm
- hair dryer (optional)
- isopropyl alcohol
- mortar and pestle
- Pasteur pipette (or other narrow bore capillary tube)
- ruler, metric
- spinach leaves (5)
- stirring rod
- tape, transparent

For each student
- gloves
- lab apron
- safety goggles

My Notes

_____

_____

_____

_____

_____

Quick Lab continued

MODIFICATION FOR INDEPENDENT (Inquiry)

Ask students to research chromatography and the use of chromatography to separate and identify plant pigments. Have them ask a question about these topics and write a hypothesis based on their question. Then have students design an experiment to test their hypothesis. Review all experimental plans for safety and feasibility and allow students to carry out approved plans. Have volunteers share their results with the class.

Answer Key

7. **Teacher Prompt** How can you keep your paper standing up? It is ok if the paper is touching the side of the beaker.

8. Accept all reasonable answers. Students should observe that some of the material in the spot moved up the filter paper and separated into new spots or streaks of different colors.

9. Sample answer: yellow-orange, green, gray, blue-green, and yellow.

10. Sample answer: Leaves look green because there is more chlorophyll in a leaf than other pigments. However, there are other pigments in a plant, not just chlorophyll.

QUICK LAB DIRECTED *Inquiry*

Investigating Plant Pigments

In this activity, you will investigate pigments in a leaf. Chlorophyll is the main pigment in plant leaves. It is chlorophyll that gives leaves their green color. Other pigments of different colors are also present in leaves. In this activity you will try to separate pigments so that you can determine which other colors are present in spinach leaves.

PROCEDURE

1 Use the mortar and pestle to crush and grind five spinach leaves. Place the ground spinach in a beaker and add just enough volume of isopropyl alcohol to cover the leaves. Stir to allow the alcohol to thoroughly wet the leaves.

2 Allow the leaves soak in the alcohol for 30 minutes (min) to make an extract. While the leaves are soaking, use the ruler and pencil to trace a line that runs horizontally along the bottom of the filter paper 2 centimeters (cm) from the bottom. This will be the starting line for your chromatograph.

3 Mix the leaf extract with the stirring rod. Then draw up a small volume of the extract in a pipette or capillary tube. Place a very small drop of the extract in the center of the pencil line you drew on the filter paper.

4 Use a hair dryer on a low setting to gently dry the spot of extract.

5 Place another drop of extract over the dried spot. Again, use the hair dryer to dry it. Repeat until the spot on the paper is dark green.

6 Allow the spot to dry completely. Wrap the non-spotted end of the paper around a pencil so that the spotted end of the paper will hang just touching the bottom of a clean, empty beaker. Adjust the paper as needed, then use a piece of tape to secure the paper to the pencil.

OBJECTIVES

- Use chromatography to separate and observe pigments present in spinach leaves.

MATERIALS

For each pair
- beakers, 250 mL (2)
- eyedropper
- filter paper strip, 12 cm × 3 cm
- hair dryer (optional)
- isopropyl alcohol
- mortar and pestle
- Pasteur pipette (or other narrow bore capillary tube)
- ruler, metric
- spinach leaves
- stirring rod
- tape, transparent

For each student
- gloves
- lab apron
- safety goggles

Quick Lab continued

7 Pour a small volume of isopropyl alcohol into the clean beaker so that the depth of the alcohol is about 1 cm. Place the filter paper into the alcohol, resting the pencil across the top of the beaker so that the filter paper is suspended in the beaker. There should be enough alcohol in the beaker to cover the bottom edge of the paper, but not deep enough to cover the spot of leaf extract.

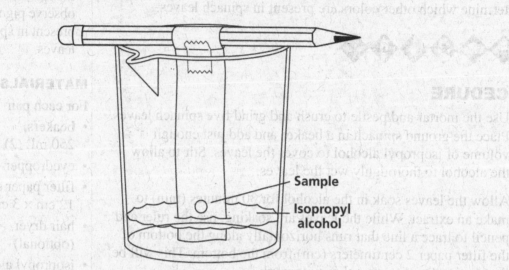

Sample

Isopropyl alcohol

8 Observe what happens. Record your observations.

_____
_____
_____

9 What colors did the green extract separate into?

_____
_____
_____

10 What can you infer about the pigments in plants based on this activity?

_____
_____
_____
_____
_____

Quick Lab continued

QUICK LAB GUIDED *Inquiry*

Observing Stomata GENERAL

👥 Student pairs

🕐 10 minutes on one day plus 20 minutes on the following day

LAB RATINGS

LESS ◄————————► MORE

Teacher Prep —

Student Setup —

Cleanup —

MATERIALS

For each pair
- cover slip
- microscope
- microscope slide
- nail polish, clear
- scissors
- spinach leaf
- tape
- water

For each student
- safety goggles

SAFETY INFORMATION

Remind students to review all safety cautions and icons before beginning this lab. Have students wear safety goggles when preparing their specimens for microscopic observations. Make sure students wash and dry their hands carefully after handling the plant leaves and nail polish.

TEACHER NOTES

In this activity, students will use a microscope to observe stomata and guard cells in spinach leaves. You may wish to review the correct way to handle and prepare slides and how to use a microscope before beginning this lab. You may wish to prepare the specimens for students to observe by coating the leaves with the nail polish and allowing them to dry overnight. You can also prepare some slides beforehand in case students damage their nail polish samples when pulling the nail polish off of the leaves. You may also wish to purchase some leaf epidermis slides from a biological supply house for students to use. This activity works well with spinach leaves, but any leaves with smooth surfaces will work. Using this method, the epidermis of the leaf is not detached; the nail polish just makes a very good impression of the surface of the leaf. When the tape and nail polish are detached and the tape is taped to a slide, the stomata can be easily seen.

Tip This activity may help students better understand the parts of a leaf. You may wish to review the structure of a leaf before beginning this activity.

Skills Focus Making Observations, Practicing Lab Techniques

My Notes

_____

_____

_____

_____

_____

MODIFICATION FOR DIRECTED *Inquiry*

Provide students with a slide of a leaf epidermis and have them observe it under the microscope. Have students draw what they see and label each part.

Answer Key

4. Check students' drawings.

   Teacher Prompt How can you adjust the microscope if the cells are not clear?

5. Check students' drawings to make sure they have correctly labeled the stomata and guard cells.

6. Accept all reasonable answers.

7. Accept all reasonable answers. If the stomata were open, then the leaf was engaged in a gas exchange.

Observing Stomata

In this activity, you will use a microscope to observe stomata and guard cells in a leaf. These cells control a plant's intake of carbon dioxide and release of water vapor.

PROCEDURE

1 Attach a 1/2" piece of tape to the underside of the leaf. (A narrow part of the tape is first folded over to make a handle for easy removal from the leaf.)

2 Paint the underside of the leaf with a coat of clear nail polish, half on the leaf and half on the tape.

3 After the nail polish dries, carefully pull the tape and the nail polish off of the leaf, taking care not to damage the thin layer of nail polish. Place the tape on a slide. The side of the nail polish that was touching the leaf should be facing up.

4 Gently add a small drop of water, and place a cover slip over the sample.

5 Use the microscope to observe the sample. Draw a sketch to show what you observe.

6 Label the stomata and guard cells on your drawing.

OBJECTIVE

- Observe the stomata and guard cells in a leaf.

MATERIALS

For each pair
- cover slip
- microscope
- microscope slide
- nail polish, clear
- scissors
- spinach leaf
- tape
- water

For each student
- safety goggles

Quick Lab continued

7 Were the guard cells swollen or not? Were the stomata open or closed? Explain.

_____

_____

8 Was the leaf exchanging gases? How can you tell?

_____

_____

_____

EXPLORATION LAB DIRECTED *Inquiry* **AND** GUIDED *Inquiry*

Fertilization in Angiosperms GENERAL

👥 Student pairs

🕐 25 minutes on Day 1, 20 minutes on Day 2

LAB RATINGS

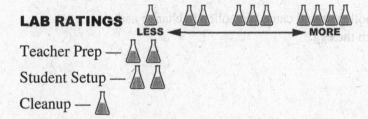

LESS ⟵⟶ MORE

Teacher Prep —

Student Setup —

Cleanup —

SAFETY INFORMATION

Remind students to review all safety cautions and icons before beginning this lab. Spilled water on the floor creates a slipping hazard, so instruct students to clean spills immediately and have paper towels available for this purpose. If any students have pollen allergies, have them wear lab gloves and a surgical mask to limit their contact with pollen. All students should wash and dry their hands after handling plants and plant parts.

TEACHER NOTES

In this activity, students will germinate some pollen grains and draw conclusions about how angiosperms are fertilized. If necessary, review with students how to prepare a wet-mount slide and how to use a microscope before beginning this lab. Try using pollen from two or more types of flowers. Conditions required for germination vary among plants and using several different types of pollen will increase the chances that students will see pollen-tube growth occur. Observations may be necessary for a longer period of time to achieve desired outcomes. This activity works well with lilies and tulips because their anthers are prominent and the pollen is easily accessible. Buttercups and bluebells are also good choices. You may wish to contact local florists to see if they will donate flowers they can no longer sell.

Tip This activity will better help students understand fertilization in angiosperms.

Student Tip Think about how angiosperms reproduce (sexual reproduction).

Skills Focus Practicing Lab Techniques, Forming Hypotheses, Making Observations

MODIFICATION FOR INDEPENDENT *Inquiry*

Ask students to describe how pollen germinates. Then, have them design an experiment in which they will germinate pollen grains. Students' procedures should include: a prediction, list of materials, step-by-step procedure that takes into account variables and any limitations, and how they are going to communicate their results. Once you have approved all reasonable procedures, have students carry out their experiments. Have students share their results with the class.

MATERIALS

For each pair

- cover slips
- cup
- eyedropper
- microscope
- microscope slides
- paper
- pencils, colored
- petri dish with cover
- pollen from flowering plant
- stirring rod
- sugar, 3.5 g
- water

For each student

- lab apron

My Notes

_____

_____

_____

_____

_____

Exploration Lab continued

Answer Key for `DIRECTED Inquiry`

ASK A QUESTION

1. Accept all reasonable answers.

FORM A PREDICTION

2. Sample answer: If I add sugar water to pollen, it will cause the pollen to change and possibly get larger so the sperm can reach the egg.

TEST THE PREDICTION

5. Check students' drawings for accuracy.
9. Check students' drawings for accuracy.

ANALYZE THE RESULTS

10. Accept all reasonable answers. Students should notice that a tube has begun to grow from the pollen grain. Depending on the power of the microscope, students may also have noticed that the pollen grains have swollen.

11. Sample answer: The tube will grow downward toward the egg.

DRAW CONCLUSIONS

12. Answers will vary depending on students' predictions.
13. Sample answer: The amount of moisture and sugar would be different from that occurring naturally, which could have affected the results.
14. Sample answer: The pollen needs to grow a tube so that the sperm will be able to reach down to the bottom of the pistil where the egg is.
15. Sample answer: If enough nutrients and moisture are available, the pollen tubes will continue to get longer.

Connect TO THE ESSENTIAL QUESTION

16. Sample answer: Plants can be characterized by the type of seeds and reproductive structures they have.

Answer Key for `GUIDED Inquiry`

ASK A QUESTION

1. Accept all reasonable answers.

FORM A PREDICTION

2. Sample answer: If I add sugar water to pollen, it will cause the pollen to change and possibly get larger so the sperm can reach the egg.

Exploration Lab continued

TEST THE PREDICTION

3. the anther

5. Check students' drawings for accuracy.

6. Sample answer: I can mix sugar and water to create sugar water and add the pollen to the mixture.

9. Check students' drawings for accuracy.

ANALYZE THE RESULTS

10. Accept all reasonable answers. Students should notice that a tube has begun to grow from the pollen grain. Depending on the power of the microscope, students may also have noticed that the pollen grains have swollen.

11. Sample answer: The tube will grow downward towards the egg.

DRAW CONCLUSIONS

12. Answers will vary depending on students' predictions.

13. Sample answer: The amount of moisture and sugar would be different from that occurring naturally, which could have affected the results.

14. Sample answer: The pollen needs to grow a tube so that the sperm will be able to reach down to the bottom of the pistil where the egg is.

15. Sample answer: If enough nutrients and moisture are available, the pollen tubes will continue to get longer.

Connect TO THE ESSENTIAL QUESTION

16. Sample answer: Plants can be characterized by the type of seeds and reproductive structures they have.

Name _____ Class _____ Date _____

Fertilization in Angiosperms

Angiosperms are flowering plants. Their flowers are made up of reproductive structures that produce seeds. A seed is a plant embryo enclosed in a protective coating. In this activity, you will set up conditions to mimic the conditions that pollen grains encounter when they land on a pistil. You will observe what happens to the pollen grains under these conditions to make inferences about reproduction in angiosperms.

PROCEDURE

ASK A QUESTION

1 In this activity you will investigate the question: How does the sperm in a pollen grain get to the egg in a pistil of a flower? Write any thoughts you have about this question.

_____

_____

_____

FORM A PREDICTION

2 Complete the following sentence: If I mimic the conditions that a pollen grain encounters when it lands on a pistil, the pollen grain will

_____

_____

_____

TEST THE PREDICTION

3 Locate the anthers on a flowering plant. Tap some pollen onto a microscope slide.

4 Place a cover slip over the pollen.

OBJECTIVES

• Induce pollen grains to begin the process of fertilization.

• Determine how pollen grains fertilize an egg.

MATERIALS

For each pair
• cover slips
• cup
• eyedropper
• microscope
• microscope slides
• paper
• pencils, colored
• petri dish with cover
• pollen from flowering plant
• stirring rod
• sugar, 3.5 g
• water

For each student
• lab apron

Exploration Lab continued

5 Using the lowest-power setting, observe the pollen under the microscope. Draw what you observe.

6 Conditions on a pistil vary from plant to plant, but in most cases, the surface is covered with a mixture of glucose and water. To mimic this, make a solution by stirring sugar into a cup of water until it dissolves. Pour enough of the sugar water into a petri dish to cover the bottom of the dish.

7 Take some pollen from the anther of your flower remaining from Step 4. Sprinkle this pollen into the petri dish. Cover the dish and leave it in a warm place overnight.

8 Make a slide of the pollen/sugar water mixture. Place a few drops of the pollen/sugar water mixture on a slide. Be sure you can see some pollen in the drops. Add a cover slip over the sample.

9 Use the microscope to observe the mixture. Draw what you observe.

ANALYZE THE RESULTS

10 **Describing Results** How did the size or shape of the pollen change from Day 1 to Day 2?

_____

_____

_____

11 **Analyzing Data** Remember that the egg is at the bottom of a flower's pistil. How might the changes you saw under the microscope help the sperm fertilize the egg?

_____

_____

_____

Exploration Lab continued

DRAW CONCLUSIONS

12 **Evaluating Hypotheses** Compare your results to your prediction. Explain whether your results support your prediction.

_____

_____

_____

_____

13 **Identifying Constraints** You added sugar water to the pollen to cause it to germinate. This gave the pollen nutrients and moisture. In nature, pollen grains get water, sugar, and other nutrients from the sticky stigma at the top of the pistil. How do you think your method may have affected your results?

_____

_____

_____

14 **Making Inferences** Picture the shape of a flower pistil. Why do you think pollen grains have to change to fertilize the egg?

_____

_____

_____

15 **Making Inferences** What do you think the pollen grains would look like in a few days?

_____

_____

_____

_____

Connect TO THE ESSENTIAL QUESTION

16 **Synthesizing Information** How can plants be characterized by the way they reproduce?

_____

_____

_____

_____

EXPLORATION LAB GUIDED *Inquiry*

Fertilization in Angiosperms

Angiosperms are flowering plants. Their flowers contain the reproductive organs each plant needs for generating seeds, which contain new plant embryos. In this activity, you will set up conditions to mimic the conditions that pollen grains encounter when they land on a pistil. You will observe what happens to the pollen grains under these conditions to make inferences about reproduction in angiosperms.

PROCEDURE

ASK A QUESTION

1 In this activity you will investigate the question: How does the sperm in a pollen grain get to the egg in a pistil of a flower? Write any thoughts you have about this question.

_____

_____

_____

_____

FORM A PREDICTION

2 Write a prediction about the effect of sugar water on pollen germination.

_____

_____

_____

_____

TEST THE PREDICTION

3 Obtain pollen. From which structure of the flower will you get the pollen?

_____

4 Use the pollen to make a microscope slide.

OBJECTIVES

• Induce pollen grains to begin the process of fertilization.

• Determine how pollen grains fertilize an egg.

MATERIALS

For each pair
• cover slips
• cup
• eyedropper
• microscope
• microscope slides
• paper
• pencils, colored
• petri dish with cover
• pollen from flowering plant
• stirring rod
• sugar, 3.5 g
• water
For each student
• lab apron

Original content Copyright © by Holt McDougal. Alterations to the original content are the responsibility of the instructor.

Exploration Lab continued

5 Using the lowest-power setting, observe the pollen under the microscope. Draw what you observe.

6 Conditions on a pistil vary from plant to plant, but in most cases, the surface is covered with a mixture of glucose and water. How can you use the available materials to set up conditions to provide this?

_____

_____

_____

7 Carry out your plan from Step 6. Let the pollen sit overnight in a warm place.

8 Make a slide of the pollen.

9 Use the microscope to observe the pollen. Draw what you observe.

ANALYZE THE RESULTS

10 **Describing Results** How did the size or shape of the pollen change from Day 1 to Day 2?

_____

_____

_____

Exploration Lab continued

⑪ Analyzing Data Remember that the egg is at the bottom of a flower's pistil. How might the changes you saw under the microscope help the sperm fertilize the egg?

_____

_____

_____

DRAW CONCLUSIONS

⑫ Evaluating Hypotheses Compare your results to your prediction. Explain whether your results support your prediction.

_____

_____

_____

_____

⑬ Identifying Constraints In nature, pollen grains get water, sugar, and other nutrients from the sticky stigma at the top of the pistil. How do you think your method may have affected your results?

_____

_____

_____

_____

⑭ Making Inferences Picture the shape of a flower pistil. Why do you think pollen grains have to change to fertilize the egg?

_____

_____

⑮ Making Inferences What do you think the pollen grains would look like in a few days?

_____

_____

_____

_____

Exploration Lab continued

Connect **TO THE ESSENTIAL QUESTION**

16 **Synthesizing Information** How can plants be characterized by the way they reproduce?

_____

_____

_____

_____

QUICK LAB DIRECTED (Inquiry)

Form and Motion GENERAL

👥 Small groups
🕐 15 minutes

LAB RATINGS

LESS ← → MORE

Teacher Prep —
Student Setup —
Cleanup —

SAFETY INFORMATION

Remind students to review all safety cautions and icons before beginning this lab.

TEACHER NOTES

In this activity, students will study animal body forms and determine how body structure relates to movement.

To prepare for this activity, you will need to collect photographs of various animals and corresponding video footage of those animals for the students to study. If you have access to student computers, you can bookmark Internet links to appropriate video footage. For example, many webpages (such as those for zoos, aquariums, and science centers) offer video from cameras mounted to live animals as well as video of live animals moving in their normal patterns.

An alternative way to conduct this lab is to provide students with live animal specimens. Examples of animals easily obtained and observed in the classroom are insects, isopods, earthworms, frogs, and fish. If live animals are to be used, appropriate steps should be taken to ensure student and animal safety.

Skills Focus Making Observations, Making Predictions

MODIFICATION FOR GUIDED (Inquiry)

Provide students with animal photographs, and ask them to describe how their animal's body structures relate to its movement. Encourage them to observe their animal in motion using the Internet or other resources. You may wish to have students present their animals and their observations.

Quick Lab continued

Answer Key

1. Answers will vary.
2. Answers will vary.
3. Answers will vary.
4. Answers will vary.

Name _____ Class _____ Date _____

Form and Motion

In this lab, you will investigate the relationships between animals' body forms and the ways in which they move.

PROCEDURE

1 Obtain a photograph of an animal from your teacher, and observe its body form. Record your observations in the following table:

OBJECTIVE
• Observe how animal form relates to motion.

MATERIALS
For each group
• animal photograph
• animal video footage

Animal:	
Characteristic	Observation
Vertebrate or invertebrate?	
Endoskeleton or exoskeleton?	
Flexible or rigid body covering?	
Flexible or rigid skeleton (if present)?	
Number of visible joints?	
Number and types (wings, legs, fins, etc.) of appendages?	

2 What observed characteristic do you predict is most important for allowing this animal to be flexible? Which is most important for allowing it to be fast? Explain your answers.

_____
_____
_____
_____
_____
_____

Quick Lab continued

❸ What observed characteristic do you predict most limits the animal's flexibility? Which most limits its speed? Explain your answers.

_____

_____

_____

_____

_____

❹ Observe your animal as it moves. How do your observations relate to your predictions?

_____

_____

_____

_____

_____

_____

_____

QUICK LAB INDEPENDENT Inquiry

Characteristics of Animals GENERAL

🐾 Individual student
🕐 25 minutes

LAB RATINGS

LESS ← → MORE

Teacher Prep —

Student Setup —

Cleanup —

MATERIALS

For each student
• paper
• pencils, colored

My Notes

_____
_____
_____
_____
_____

TEACHER NOTES

In this activity, students will use paper and colored pencils to design and sketch a fictional animal that shares the five characteristics of most animals. Students will brainstorm and sketch the animal, and then they will be asked to identify and label the specific characteristics of their animal.

Tip Some students may need to see an example of a "new" animal in order to get started.

Skills Focus Constructing Models, Applying Concepts

MODIFICATION FOR GUIDED Inquiry

Provide students with the five characteristics of most animals. Then challenge students to brainstorm and sketch fictional animals with these characteristics.

Answer Key

1. Sample answer: Most animals have the following characteristics: multicellular, reproduce sexually, have specialized parts, have the ability to move, and eat other organisms to get energy.

2. Accept all reasonable answers.

3. Accept all reasonable designs. Students should label and describe the features of their fictitious animal that address the five basic characteristics of most animals.

4. Accept all reasonable answers.

5. Accept all reasonable answers.

Name _____ Class _____ Date _____

Characteristics of Animals

In this lab you will brainstorm and sketch a fictional animal that has all of the characteristics of most animals that exist in the real world.

PROCEDURE

1 List five characteristics that most animals have in common with each other.

_____

_____

_____

_____

2 Brainstorm and describe a fictional animal that shares the characteristics you listed in Step 1.

_____

_____

_____

_____

3 Draw a sketch of your animal on a separate piece of paper. Be sure to clearly identify and label the specific features that address the five characteristics that your animal has in common with real-world animals.

OBJECTIVES

- Identify the characteristics that most animals share.
- Design a fictional animal with real-world characteristics.

MATERIALS

For each student
- paper
- pencils, colored

Quick Lab continued

4 Describe where your animal lives, what it eats, and how it moves.

_____

_____

_____

_____

_____

_____

5 Is your animal a vertebrate or invertebrate? Explain.

_____

_____

_____

_____

_____

QUICK LAB GUIDED Inquiry

At a Snail's Pace GENERAL

👥 Small groups
🕐 30 minutes

LAB RATINGS

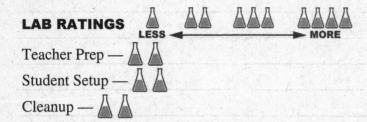

LESS ←――――――→ MORE

Teacher Prep —
Student Setup —
Cleanup —

SAFETY INFORMATION

Remind students to review all safety cautions and icons before beginning this lab. Emphasize the importance of treating lab animals with care and respect so that they do not harm the animals in any way. Students should wash their hands thoroughly before and after handling the snails.

MATERIALS

For each group
• books
• flashlight
• marker, permanent
• picture frame,
  20 cm × 20 cm
• ruler
• snail
• tape, masking
For each student
• safety goggles

TEACHER NOTES

In this activity students will develop a simple experiment to test how snails respond to light. Because snails prefer to travel up an incline, it is advisable to conduct the experiment on a surface that can be held at an angle to the horizontal. This will encourage snail movement so that the snail's response to light can be observed. When students direct a light on the snail, they should observe that the snail moves away from the light. This response is called phototaxis, or light sensitivity. More precisely, it means movement in response to light ("taxis" means movement).

My Notes

_____
_____
_____
_____
_____

Either land or aquatic snails may be used, but the results are more apparent with land snails. Have extra snails available in the event that some snails will not move. If using aquatic snails, prepare aquariums or tubs of water to keep them moist during the lab.

The picture frame provides a glass surface that can be safely handled by students; however, other surfaces may be used as long as they are smooth and students can observe the trail left by their snail.

Tip Turn off the lights in the classroom so that students can better control the amount and direction of light shining on the snail. Encourage students to test the snail's response to light from different light source locations.

Student Tip Snails prefer to travel upward along an incline. To encourage snail movement, consider placing the snail at the bottom of a ramp.

Skills Focus Making Observations, Analyzing Results

Quick Lab continued

MODIFICATION FOR DIRECTED Inquiry

Have students prop one end of the picture frame on a stack of books to create a ramp. Have students place a strip of masking tape near the base of the frame and label this position "Initial Position." Then have students place the snail at the initial position and shine the flashlight onto the snail from the base of the ramp. On a separate sheet of paper, students can sketch the direction of the beam of light and the path along which the snail traveled.

Have students shine the light for 5 minutes and then use a ruler to measure the total distance that the snail travels. Then, have students repeat the test once more by shining the flashlight on the snail at a different angle up the ramp. Finally, have students observe a controlled test by not shining any light on the snail at all for 5 minutes. Remind students that they should control as many variables as possible for each trial. For example, they should shine the light on the snail for the same amount of time, and they should hold the flashlight at the same distance from the snail during every test.

Answer Key

1. Students should make a reasonable prediction about how they think the snails movement will relate to light and dark conditions.

2. Accept all reasonable answers. Students' procedures should list the variables and detail a plan for their measurements and observations, including how they will record their data. **Teacher Prompt** What will you use as a control in this experiment? How could you vary the light source?

3. Accept all reasonable answers.

4. Sample answer: Yes, the snail seemed to move away from the light source even when it was directed at the snail from two different locations. Also, the snail did not move at all when no light was shining. So, I think that snails respond to light by moving away from it.

5. Sample answer: Based on my observations, I think snails are more likely to be found in dark places. In the experiment, the snail moved away from the light source and stopped when it was in the dark.

Name _____ Class _____ Date _____

QUICK LAB GUIDED *Inquiry*

At a Snail's Pace

In this lab, you will design an experiment to observe how snails respond to light. Always wash your hands before and after handling snails, and only handle snails by touching their shells. (Touching the soft tissue of a snail can harm the snail). To pick up a snail, wet your fingers and carefully lift up the snail from the front to the back.

PROCEDURE

1 How do you think snails move in response to light versus darkness? Make a prediction about how you think snails will respond to each of these conditions.

_____

_____

2 Work with your group to develop a list of procedures that you will follow in order to test your prediction. What are the dependent and independent variables? How will you measure and record your observations? What are the variables that you will control? Conduct your investigation once your instructor has approved your set of procedures.

_____

_____

_____

_____

_____

_____

OBJECTIVES
- Observe how snails respond to light.
- Identify the relationship between light stimulus and animal behavior.

MATERIALS
- books
- flashlight
- marker, permanent
- picture frame, 20 cm × 20 cm
- ruler
- snail
- tape, masking

For each student
- safety goggles

Quick Lab continued

③ Do your data support your prediction? Explain your answer.

_____

_____

_____

_____

_____

④ Was there a relationship between light and the snail's movement?
If so, describe this relationship.

_____

_____

_____

⑤ Based on your results, are you more likely to find snails in cool, dark places
or in warm, bright places? Explain your answer in relation to your results.

_____

_____

_____

QUICK LAB `DIRECTED` Inquiry

Modeling Predator-Prey Scenarios `GENERAL`

👥 Small groups
🕐 30 minutes

LAB RATINGS

LESS ◄————————► MORE

Teacher Prep —
Student Setup —
Cleanup —

MATERIALS
For each group
• balls, small (12)

My Notes

_____

_____

_____

_____

_____

SAFETY INFORMATION

Remind students to review all safety cautions and icons before beginning this lab. Students should use caution if walking near a group that is rolling balls; remind students that they should roll the balls responsibly so that they do not injure other students. Students should never throw the balls through the air.

TEACHER NOTES

In this activity, students will work in small groups to model predator-prey scenarios. Students in the group will roll balls, representing prey, toward another student representing a predator. The "predator" will attempt to catch the rolled balls. As the number of balls rolled at one time increases, students should observe that the percentage of prey captured declines. From this, they will observe how the percentage of prey captured relates to the number of prey in the group approaching the predator. They will draw conclusions about how animals traveling in groups can be a defensive behavior.

Be sure to clear out (or reserve) open floor space for student groups to conduct the investigation. Each group will need approximately 2 meters × 1 meter of floor space.

Tip Instruct students who are not actively rolling or catching balls during a trial within their group to help count the number of balls captured.

Student Tip Rotate roles in the group often to prevent any one predator from gaining a "learning advantage" over the others.

Skills Focus Making Predictions, Analyzing Data

MODIFICATION FOR `GUIDED` Inquiry

Students should complete the activity as described, but they should be challenged to create their own data table rather than using the one provided in the student datasheet.

Quick Lab continued

Answer Key

3. Sample answer:

PREDATOR-PREY CAPTURES

Number of prey in group	Trial	Number of captures	Percent of prey capture: (captures/prey) × 100 %
1	1	1	
	2	1	
	3	1	
	4	1	
	5	1	
	6	1	
	7	1	
	8	1	
	9	1	
	10	0	
	11	1	
	12	1	
average (total sum/12)		11/12	92%
2	1	2	
	2	2	
	3	1	
	4	1	
	5	1	
	6	2	
average (total sum/12)		9/12	75%

Quick Lab continued

Number of prey in group	Trial	Number of captures	Percent of prey capture: (captures/prey) × 100 %
3	1	2	
	2	1	
	3	1	
	4	2	
average (total sum/12)		6/12	50%
4	1	2	
	2	0	
	3	1	
average (total sum/12)		3/12	25%

4. Accept all reasonable answers.

8. Sample answer: My prediction was correct. The data suggest that the percentage of prey caught decreases as the group size increases.

9. Sample answer: I think animals travel in groups to reduce their chances of being caught by a predator. This is a defense behavior.

10. Sample answer: buffalo and fish

QUICK LAB DIRECTED Inquiry

Modeling Predator-Prey Scenarios

In this lab, you will explore how the size of a traveling group of animals relates to predator attacks on the group. Members of your group will roll balls across the floor to model prey as they travel. Another member of the group, representing the predator, will attempt to catch the rolling balls. You will observe how the amount of catches relates to the number of balls rolled at one time.

PROCEDURE

❶ Designate one student in the group to act as the predator. The predator should sit on the floor in an open space.

❷ Designate another student in the group to act as the prey. That student should receive all 12 balls and should sit 2 meters from the predator. The prey will roll the balls, one at a time, toward the predator. The predator should attempt to catch the balls. Record the number of catches for each trial in the table below.

OBJECTIVES

• Model how predators attack prey in different-sized groups.

• Recognize a relationship between group size and survival rate.

MATERIALS

For each group
• balls, small (12)

PREDATOR-PREY CAPTURES

Number of prey in group	Trial	Number of captures	Percent of prey capture: (captures/prey) × 100 %
1	1		
	2		
	3		
	4		
	5		
	6		
	7		
	8		
	9		
	10		
	11		
	12		
average (total sum/12)			

Name _____ Class _____ Date _____

Quick Lab continued

Number of prey in group	Trial	Number of captures	Percent of prey capture: (captures/prey) × 100 %
2	1		
	2		
	3		
	4		
	5		
	6		
average (total sum/12)			
3	1		
	2		
	3		
	4		
average (total sum/12)			
4	1		
	2		
	3		
average (total sum/12)			

❸ Compute the average number of captures and the percentage of prey captures.

❹ Predict what will happen to the percentage of prey captures if the number of balls rolled at one time increases.

_____

_____

_____

❺ Repeat Steps 1–3, only this time, have two students acting as the prey. Each student should receive six balls. The prey should roll the balls at the same time, repeating six times until all of the balls have been rolled.

❻ Repeat Steps 1–3, this time with three students acting as the prey. Each student will have four balls. The prey should roll the balls at the same time, repeating four times until all of the balls have been rolled.

Quick Lab continued

7 Repeat Steps 1–3, this time with four students acting as the prey. Each student will have three balls. The prey should roll the balls at the same time, repeating three times until all of the balls have been rolled.

8 What do your data suggest about the size of a group of prey in relation to predator attacks? Was your original prediction correct?

_____

_____

_____

9 Based on your results, why do you think that some animals travel in groups?

_____

_____

10 Work with your group to brainstorm two examples of animals that travel in large groups.

_____

_____